Risk Classification by Means of Clustering

Schriften zum Controlling, Finanz- und Risikomanagement

Herausgegeben von Andreas Brieden, Thomas Hartung,
Bernhard Hirsch und Andreas Schüler

Band 4

PETER LANG

Frankfurt am Main · Berlin · Bern · Bruxelles · New York · Oxford · Wien

Bernhard Christian Kübler

Risk Classification
by Means of Clustering

PETER LANG
Internationaler Verlag der Wissenschaften

Bibliographic Information published by the Deutsche Nationalbibliothek
The Deutsche Nationalbibliothek lists this publication in the Deutsche Nationalbibliografie; detailed bibliographic data is available in the internet at http://dnb.d-nb.de.

Zugl.: München, Univ. der Bundeswehr., Diss., 2009

D 706
ISSN 1867-027X
ISBN 978-3-631-59759-0

© Peter Lang GmbH
Internationaler Verlag der Wissenschaften
Frankfurt am Main 2010
All rights reserved.

www.peterlang.de

Vorwort

Die vorliegende Dissertation entstand während meiner Tätigkeit als wissenschaftlicher Mitarbeiter an der Professur für Statistik, insbesondere Risikomanagement an der Universität der Bundeswehr München.

Mein Dank gilt meinem Doktorvater Herrn Professor Dr. Andreas Brieden, der durch seine erstklassige Betreuung entscheidend zum Gelingen der Arbeit beigetragen hat. Herrn Professor Dr. Thomas Hartung danke ich für die Übernahme des Zweitgutachtens.

Besonderer Dank gilt meinen Eltern, denen diese Arbeit auch gewidmet ist. Sie haben durch ihre großzügige Unterstützung die Anfertigung dieser Arbeit ermöglicht.

Contents

List of Figures

List of Abbreviations

a.s.	almost surely
CC	Cross classification
cf.	compare
e.g.	for example
fig.	figure
i.e.	that is
i.i.d.	independent and identically distributed
MAE	Mean absolute error
MC	Multidimensional credibility-based algorithm
MSE	Mean squared error
TWSS	Total within group sum of squares
vs.	versus
w.l.o.g.	without loss of generality

Chapter 1

Introduction

1.1 Exploratory Focus

The crucial aspect of pricing insurance premiums is – compared to other products such as cars or computers – that the cost of the good protection/insurance is not known beforehand; the cost (namely the claim sizes) for the insurance company will not be known until some date in the future. Thus, insurers have to develop alternative approaches to determine adequate prices for their products. Accurate pricing is a critical issue for at least two reasons. First, the *overall* level of premiums has to guarantee safety and profit objectives: Too low premiums do not ensure the insurer's liability to cover the claims and thus guarantee its solvency or are not able to ensure the compliance of certain profit margins, whereas too high premiums banish customers. A liquid insurer is not only important to the insurer itself but also to the policyholders since they are given the guarantee to receive payments in case of a claim event. Second, it is particularly important to get the *relative* premium structure right. An important aspect within this context is **adverse selection**: If an insurer charges too little for high risk groups and too much for low risk groups, it will eventually lose low risk customers and gain high risk customers (such customer fluctuations are very likely since insurance markets have become highly competitive in the past decades, see [Völ08]). This obviously has a substantial influence on portfolio performance as the high risks cost too much and yield too low accruals of funds and the low risk groups are likely to terminate their policies. Increasing the overall level of premiums to raise profitability again even worsens the situation as it compounds the drawback of too low and too high premiums. This leads to a spiral of losing low risk customers and attracting high risk customers. Thus the relative levels of premiums have to be fixed correctly in order to be competitive, and this is the main aspect of statistical approaches to premium pricing.

All ideas being developed in the course of this investigation are valid for all branches of non-life insurance. Typically, we shall illustrate our arguments by examples from motor third party insurance since tariffs within this branch partition their portfolios to a – compared to other branches of insurance – greater extent and since we shall carry out an empirical analysis related to car insurance. So our first observation regarding adverse selection relates to (German) motor insurance as well, cf. [Sie71]: As is known, the Nazi regime intended to increase the level of motorization of the German population. Against this background, it enforced a uniform tariff[1] ("flat rate") for motor insurance.[2] As the civil road traffic almost vanished due to the outbreak of war in 1939, one cannot judge whether or not this uniform tariff would have coped with the situation before 1939. After the war, the existing uniform tariff had been adapted by insurance firms initially. However, it turned out quite early that one had to charge increased contributions. The problem of adverse selection described above was compounded by such an increasement. The differentation of rates in motor insurance has become inevitable.

Having noticed the necessity to install a risk-differentiating

---

[1] In fact, there was a very course differentation according to *type of vehicle, power* and *insured sum*

[2] Legal foundation: *Pflichtversicherungsgesetz*

tariff, we pose the question how this can be achieved. The key is to make use of the (strong) law of large numbers. In our context, we think of random variables X_i ($i \in \mathbb{N}$) as **claim sizes**. Before we formulate the laws of large numbers, let us review two important concepts of convergence coming up in this context: *P-almost sure convergence* of the sequence $(X_n)_{n \in \mathbb{N}}$ of real random variables on a probability space $(\Omega, \mathcal{A}, P)$ towards a real random variable X on $(\Omega, \mathcal{A}, P)$ means

$$P\{\lim_{n \to \infty} X_n = X\} = 1$$

and *P-stochastic convergence* means

$$\lim_{n \to \infty} P\{|X_n - X| \geq \varepsilon\} = 0 \quad (\varepsilon > 0).$$

Definition 1.1.1 *Let $(X_n)_{n \in \mathbb{N}}$ be a sequence of integrable real random variables on a probability space $(\Omega, \mathcal{A}, P)$.*

(i) $(X_n)_{n \in \mathbb{N}}$ *is said to satisfy the* **weak law of large numbers** *if*

$$\lim_{n \to \infty} \frac{1}{n} \sum_{i=1}^{n} (X_i - E(X_i)) = 0$$

holds in the sense of P-stochastic convergence.

(ii) $(X_n)_{n \in \mathbb{N}}$ *is said to satisfy the* **strong law of large numbers** *if*

$$\lim_{n \to \infty} \frac{1}{n} \sum_{i=1}^{n} (X_i - E(X_i)) = 0 \qquad P - a.s.$$

Of course, the implication (ii) $\Longrightarrow$ (i) holds. There are various conditions which can be shown to be sufficient for the occurrence of a law of large numbers, cf. [Bau02]. The most prominent results are the theorems of Kolmogorov, the theorem of Khinchin and the theorem of Etemadi,[3] according to which the random variables X_i ($i \in \mathbb{N}$) particularly are assumed to be **identically distributed**.

---

[3] We mention another sufficient condition in the so called *production law of the insurance technology* in Chapter 3.

Proposition 1.1.2 (Khinchin) *If the sequence $(X_n)_{n \in \mathbb{N}}$ of integrable and pairwise uncorrelated random variables with variances $V(X_n)$ obeys*

$$\lim_{n \to \infty} \frac{1}{n^2} \sum_{i=1}^{n} V(X_i) = 0,$$

it satisfies the weak law of large numbers.

Proof. See [Bau02]. □

We now state a very general condition.

Proposition 1.1.3 (Etemadi) *Each sequence $(X_n)_{n \in \mathbb{N}}$ of real, integrable, identically distributed and pairwise independent random variables obeys the strong law of large numbers.*

Proof. See [Ete81]. □

Actually, there are two pertinent theorems of Kolmogorov. We cite that one requiring identically distributed random variables and thus providing a link to cluster analysis; it follows immediately from the theorem of Etemadi.

Corollary 1.1.4 (Kolmogorov) *Each independent sequence $(X_n)_{n \in \mathbb{N}}$ of real i.i.d. random variables satisfies the strong law of large numbers.*

Aiming to make use of these statements, one has to lay the foundations for applying them. For instance, one of the (sufficient) conditions which is common to all stated theorems is to consider (a) infinitely many (b) identically distributed random variables (the law of large numbers is a statement on convergence, i.e. the behaviour of a finite number of risks is not decisive, instead, a sequence of infinitely many risks is required). **Cluster analysis** is an adequate aid to generate reasonably *large* families of risks which we assume to have the *same distribution*. By considering such – in some degree – large families ("clusters") of

14

identically distributed risks we expect the strong law of large numbers to work. If we would like to make a statement on the expected claim size of a risk (this quantity serves as fundament of many premium calculation principles), the laws of large numbers justify to look at a (sufficiently large) group of risks having the same distribution. We hope to obtain such a group by a suitable clustering. So in other words, our considerations mean to raise the statistical basis for estimation purposes. We will continue discussing these ideas in conjunction with determining suitable collective sizes later on.

So far, we have been concerned with the *expected value* of the claims size distribution. We will see, however, that some premium principles such as the variance principle require to know *higher moments* of the claim size distribution as well. The so-called quantile principle even requires the actuary to know the *entire* claim size distribution. To deal with these issues, the **Glivenko-Cantelli theorem** (see [GS77]), an application of the strong law of large numbers, produces relief. According to the Glivenko-Cantelli theorem, the distribution function F (which is independent of n) of X_n can be determined approximately in the sense of P-a.s. uniform convergence by means of samples, i.e. by realizations of the sequence $(X_n)_{n\in\mathbb{N}}$ and the corresponding empirical distributions. Observe that the latter statement again requires a sequence $(X_n)_{n\in\mathbb{N}}$ of i.i.d. real random variables, so performing a cluster analysis is appropriate here, too.

Having recognized that the way to generate large homogeneous risk groups leads over the law of large numbers and hence via cluster analysis, we pose the question in which manner one ought to cluster in order to obtain preferable (or in some sense "optimal") classification results. This question constitutes the subject matter of our analysis. There are indefinitely many methods to design a classification scheme assigning homogeneous risks the same tariff class. We put forward arguments in favour of a particular approach to be developed in the course of this research. Our new proposal will be referred to as MC (*multidimensional credibility-based classifica-*

tion algorithm). MC decisively exceeds currently used *cross classification* techniques – referred to as CC – and gives the applicant widest latitude to choose a variety of parameters such as the number of tariff classes. A particular feature of the MC is its generalizing CC methods: It can be shown that CC turns out to be just a special case of MC. Other significant benefits of MC compared to CC are to be discussed. Conceivable shortcomings of CC such as empty cells are detected to be unable to emerge within the framework of MC. By installing a classification scheme based on MC, meaningful subdivisions of a collective can be generated even when the number of tariff classes is a prime number. Additionally, an empirical investigation is carried out which eventually illustrates the superiority of MC by means of a concrete collective. Taking all theoretical and empirical results into account, there are very demonstrative reasons to choose MC from the infinite set of possibilities which exist in order to partition an insurance collective.

To complete these introductory remarks and to underline the general importance of categorizing (economic) data, we give a brief tour d'horizon where cluster analytical techniques already have been implemented successfully in the field of business and risk management. Eventually, insights gained in the following discussion can help to identify further application possibilities of MC.

1.2 Economic Incentive and Examples of Classification

This section provides a general discussion of the necessity of classification activities in economics, business and risk management. We also state some combinatorial facts justifying the need for cluster analytical techniques. Moreover, we cover the most prominent examples of fields in which clustering techniques have been successfully applied by reviewing selected papers.

1.2.1 On the Relevance of Classification in Economics

In business, specifically risk management, one often has to deal with a great multitude of objects, e.g. persons, documents, financial assets, insured risks and so forth. Decision makers who have to work on the data may be unable to see the wood for the trees. In such cases pattern recognition within the data, i.e. the aggregation of similar objects into homogeneous classes turns out to be a significant issue. Forming categories may help to reveal the structure of the data and to discover relationships within the data. A simplified representation of a complex body of data contributes to get an improved understanding and a better orientation. Obviously, it is more convenient to deal with a manageable set of only few groups rather than with an unordered set of many objects. Generally speaking, appropriate data simplification by considering only few classes saves time and generates economic benefits.

From a mathematical viewpoint, the classification task in statistical applications poses a combinatorial optimization problem. This explains the need for systematic procedures and algorithms to obtain an – at least relatively – optimal (in the sense of some target function) classification result. As an example, take a look at the number of possibilities to sort 50 objects into 5 groups. There are as many as $S(50,5) \approx 7.401 \cdot 10^{32}$ (referred to as *Stirling number of the second kind*) ways, an astonishing quantity. To make things even worse, the problem is compounded by the fact that normally the number of groups is not known in advance. In this scenario, the number of ways of grouping 50 objects amounts to about $B(50) \approx 1.857 \cdot 10^{47}$ (referred to as *50th Bell number*). These values demonstrate in a striking way that total enumeration and evaluation (with respect to some chosen objective function) of so many classification results is not possible, even when high speed computers are used to calculate the values of the target function. Moreover, real data sets like credit portfolios are often in the region of several hundreds of thousands objects, which implies tremendous numbers of possible classifications.

Having reduced the diversity of a given data set to a manageable set of categories, this result may be used as an aid for developing a classification scheme. In this context, we shall use the term classification to describe the assignment of an additional object to its proper place in an already established set of groups. This is relevant when a bank classifies applicants for a credit into given classes of good or bad risks, see Examples 1.2.1. Eventually, by classifying a new object into the scheme one hopes to be able to make predictions about properties which have not been reported – in the case of a credit applicant, the risk quality (creditworthiness) is inferred from the reported characteristics annual income, type of occupation and so forth.

Using homogeneous groups in order to achieve better forecasting results is quite customary. To clarify this point, let us assume that the relationship between two or more variables is to be investigated, e.g. by a regression analysis. It may occur – in the case of a *structural change* – that this relationship is not stable over all observations (variable parameter values). Therefore, a given sample of observations is normally being split up such that within the subgroups the same relationship between the variables holds, i.e. the parameter values are constant. The same principle applies to dealing with heteroscedastic disturbances, where the data set is to be partitioned into two groups both of which are assumed to have constant variances of the disturbance terms.

More generally, [EG70] and [EG71] work out three reasons for classifying economic data into "meaningful" subsets:

(a) to isolate units that act in a similar way

(b) to hold the effect of an omitted variable onto other variables constant

(c) to obtain a homogeneous interrelation between the variables included in a model.

18

One can show that homogeneous groups are in many cases a necessary foundation in order to test economic and financial statements. Particularly as far as the social sciences are concerned, researchers very often face the problem of isolating the effect of certain variables. Moreover, the authors show by means of an empirical study that such a homogeneous grouping leads to better forecasts than a more heterogeneous grouping does.

1.2.2 Application Areas of Cluster Analysis

To receive an impression of the importance and successful implementation of clustering techniques in business and related fields, let us take a look at some typical situations where classification problems arise. For numerous other examples the reader ought to refer to [SS77], [Vog75] and [Wei87]. Here, we devote our considerations to applications in risk management.

Examples 1.2.1 (a) In the **insurance industry**, a crucial problem is to set risk adequate premiums. Premiums must cover the amount of expected claims and ensure a certain level of profitability, but they must not be so high such that market share is jeopardized. It is obviously neither possible to offer each risk an individual contract nor to offer one single contract (hence to require the same premium) to all policy holders. However, similar risks can be grouped together and then be offered the same contract. Similarity of risks is based upon variables such as demographic factors, driving record and driving experience; these attributes are considered predictors of claim cost.

Accurate classification is an important issue in the insurance industry: Misclassifying good risks and charging too high premiums result in termination of these policies and the cost of the loss of these premiums, so the company prices itself out of the market, whereas misclassifying bad risks and charging too low premiums result in

19

expected net payments (losses) associated with these policies. Hence, both cases of misclassification lead to a financial loss. Having categorized a given portfolio into homogeneous risk classes, premium calculation can be based directly upon the found results, e.g. by applying premium principles (roughly speaking, a premium principle is a map that assigns each risk a suitable premium) to each of the risk classes. The benefits of employing a clustering approach over other premium forecast methods such as regression analysis (see [ST87]) are described in [SWB00] and [YSWB01].

(b) The goal of **portfolio theory** is to select securities from a wide investment universe to generate μ-σ-optimal (in the sense of
Markowitz) investment decisions. Occasionally, attempts are made to arrange securities in similar categories; such classifications may support portfolio managers in their portfolio-selection-decision.
[Jen71] clusters shares of 113 major companies listed on the New York Stock Exchange (N.Y.S.E.) using 9 characteristics such as capital structure, dividends, earnings data and some specific stock market perfomances on the basis of the years 1949-53. Depending upon the investment strategy, portfolio managers can find similar shares to substitute for one another in narrowly focussed portfolios or, alternatively, find different shares for diversified portfolios. Additionally, observing the clusters in the period 1954-65 (ex-post-analysis), different performances are to be noticed. This particularly means that some clusters perform better than the stock market average; that knowledge can be utilized by portfolio managers to improve profits for their clients.

[FP80] formulate an alternative portfolio optimization problem based not on "actual" securities but on "quasi-securities" – clusters of (in terms of return parameters) homogeneous securities. Interestingly, portfolios resulting from the alternative approach using such synthetic quasi-securities are shown to have a better ex-post-performance than port-folios resulting from the corresponding standard portfolio optimization model.

(c) Let us now focus on **credit scoring**, see [HH97] and [Ede92]. Predicting creditworthiness is a core activity of banks, building societies, retailers and so forth. Before granting a loan to a particular credit applicant, the creditor would like to determine how likely the repayments of that credit user default, hence to classify him or her into a good or a bad risk category. Credit scoring is the term to describe statistical methods used for this purpose. Accurate classification is substantial not only for the creditor who should avoid probable losses, but also for the credit applicant avoiding overcommitment. Typical characteristics – in this context referred to as *predictor variables* – used in the classification process are the applicant's annual income, type of occupation, home status (e.g. owner, tenant), age, marital status, time at present address and time with employer. [HH97] describe which variable selection procedures are commonly implemented in credit scoring, namely (i) the use of expert knowledge, (ii) the use of stepwise statistical procedures and (iii) selecting individual characteristics "by using a measure of the difference beween the distributions of the good and bad risks on that characteristic". Techniques in order to identify groups of good and bad risks are – besides cluster analysis – judgmental methods and statistical scoring methods such as regression analysis, discriminant analysis, decision trees and expert systems.

[Lun92] classifies a random sample of credit applicants (private persons). The clusters can easily be identified as school leavers, professionals, pensioners and so forth. Examining the results, this classification yields 6 subgroups, well-distinguished in terms of credit score: Each applicant is rated by a score ranging from 1 (lowest degree of creditworthiness) up to 5 points (highest degree of creditworthiness); and an index for a particular class is given by the

21

ratio of the average credit score of the given class to the overall average credit score. The found index values for the 6 categories range from 0.06 to 3.23, indicating quite different creditworthiness levels of the clusters. To give a concrete example for the discrepancy of the cluster structures: Only 1.7% of type 2's members fall in the highest score group 5, whereas 72.5% of type 4's members fall in the highest rating class. This underlines the ability of the clustering approach to indicate different qualities of creditworthiness, the predictive strength of this tool is obvious. Apparently, these results can be used to establish overall profitable strategies for different groups of customers. For instance, groups deemed creditworthy could be offered other financial products at an earlier stage, whereas groups deemed not creditworthy could be either rejected or offered alternative credit products. Moreover, such segmentations allow to target customers more directly: The category school leaver is certainly more interested in personal loans for cars than in home improvement loans, which may be interesting for professionals. [Web96] and [Hof99] address such "marketing activities" of banks and insurance groups beyond the pure question of creditworthiness by employing fuzzy clustering techniques. Such segmentations allow to better focus on individual consumers' requirements and to offer each segment suitable financial products and thus are essentially important for any strategic planning in this area.

(d) [Jaj98] reports on applications in **corporate finance**, particularly as far as *rating* (analysis of the financial condition of a firm) is concerned. For rating purposes, it is customary to use the following 5 groups of variables: liquidity-, debt management-, activity-, profitability and market ratios. [FIM01] investigate the creditworthiness of firms, more precisely, they are concerned with **internal rating models** (i.e. with models which are beyond classification systems of rating agencies such as Moody's or Standard & Poor's). The need for such internal rating systems stems from the calculation of regulatory capital requirements proposed by the *Basel Committee on Banking Supervision* in January 2001. A logit model is used to predict a firm's *probability of default* (dependent variable). The independent variables included in the model are balance sheet variables related to profitability, liquidity, leverage and financial structure. Additionally, two variables regarding tension in credit lines are included. Subsequently, cluster analysis is applied to assign borrowers to each class – of course, this assignment is based on the estimated probability of default. In practice, [KW01] finds that major German banks typically have from 6 to 10 such rating classes. A particular benefit of applying cluster analysis is to produce reliable measures of the average default probability for each risk grade. This is due to relatively homogeneous underlying populations of borrowers.

We give another example related to corporate finance. **Asset-backed securitization** has become an important refinancing technique and particularly an instrument for credit risk transfer for financial institutions, see [WHP03]. Against the background of recent developments in the financial markets, their crisis in 2007/2008 and the collapse of financial institutions due to their investing in asset-backed securities (ABS), we briefly look at that class of securities, and we mention a special condition for the securitization of claims and credits. When banks securitize their claims, they typically package *homogeneous* units. Generally, the pooling is due to generating a sufficient transaction volume. According to [RHSS07], the reasons for pooling only homogeneous assets are:

- There is no complete flow of information from the originator (bank) of ABS to the investors. The investor is given merely information regarding the pooled positions made anonymous. No information is given regarding particular claims or regarding particular borrowers. By obtaining a certain level of homogeneity, the quality of the claims contained in the pool does not vary too much.

- Consequently, homogeneity allows the originator to generate cash flows which can be prognosticated very well.

Obtaining such homogeneous packages of claims or credits has opened another wide field for implementing clustering techniques. In fact, credits allowed to companies are hardly to securitize since sets of such credits usually are fairly heterogeneous. This lack of homogeneity had the following consequence: To allow for the securitization of firm credits, a new type of asset-backed securities, namely collateralized loan obligations (CLOs) had to be created, cf. [RHSS07].

1.3 Notation

In what follows, we assume a probability space $(\Omega, \mathcal{A}, P)$ and model a collective consisting of n insurable risks as a family of nonnegative random (i.e. measurable) variables $X_i : (\Omega, \mathcal{A}) \longrightarrow (\mathbb{R}_+, \mathcal{B}_+)$ $(1 \leq i \leq n)$ where $\mathcal{B}_+$ denotes the trace of the σ-algebra $\mathcal{B}$ of Borel subsets of $\mathbb{R}$ in $\mathbb{R}_+ := \{x \in \mathbb{R} \,|\, x \geq 0\}$. Recall that the Borel σ-algebra $\mathcal{B}$ is induced by all open subsets of $\mathbb{R}$; its *trace* in $\mathbb{R}_+$ is defined by $\mathcal{B}_+ := \mathbb{R}_+ \cap \mathcal{B} := \{\mathbb{R}_+ \cap B \,|\, B \in \mathcal{B}\}$. The occurrences and sizes of claims usually are viewed as idealized random experiments. For $B \in \mathcal{B}_+$ we write

$$\{X \in B\} := X^{-1}(B) := \{\omega \in \Omega \mid X(\omega) \in B\}$$

and $P\{X \in B\}$ for the corresponding probability. We now clearify some terms appearing frequently in the text.

Definition 1.3.1 *Let X be a – nonnegative – real random variable on a probability space $(\Omega, \mathcal{A}, P)$.*

*(i) The **expectation** of X is given by*

$$E(X) := \int X \, dP.$$

*(ii) If I is countable and $\Omega = \bigcup_{i \in I} B_i$ is a decomposition of Ω into pairwise disjoint events $B_i \in \mathcal{A}$ with probabilities $P(B_i) > 0$, the **conditional expectation** of X **under the hypothesis** B_i is*

$$E_{B_i}(X) := P(B_i)^{-1} \int_{B_i} X \, dP.$$

*(iii) If X is integrable, the **variance** of X is given by*

$$V(X) := E\left((X - E(X))^2\right).$$

The number
$$\sigma_X := \sqrt{V(X)}$$

*is referred to as **standard deviation** of X. Occasionally, the expression $\sigma(X)$ to denote the standard deviation is used as well.*

(iv) For two integrable real random variables X and Y whose product is integrable,

$$cov(X, Y) := E(XY) - E(X)E(Y)$$

*is the **covariance** of X and Y.*

*(v) The image measure P_X of X with respect to P is referred to as **distribution** of X under P, i.e.*

$$P_X(B) = P\{X \in B\} \quad (B \in \mathcal{B}_+).$$

In many applications, one often considers either *discrete* or *continuous* random variables. However, as far as our applications are concerned, insurance risks are neither purely discrete nor purely continuous random variables, but a kind of "combination": There is a considerable probability on zero (i.e. no claim) and there is zero probability for values larger than the maximum sum insured. Restricting ourselves to values (claim sizes) between zero and the maximum sum insured, we may assume that risks can be modelled by continuous random variables. We now develop a simple example of how the distribution P_X of an unbounded claim size X could be modelled, namely

$$P_X = p\delta_0 + (1-p)Exp(\alpha)$$

where δ_0 denotes the Dirac measure (on $2^{\mathbb{R}}$) at 0, i.e. $\delta_0(\{0\}) = 1$ and $\delta_0(\mathbb{R} \setminus \{0\}) = 0$, $0 < p < 1$ and $Exp(\alpha)$ is the exponential distribution (with parameter $\alpha > 0$). Thus P_X is indeed a probability measure on $\mathbb{R}$. Particularly, our model has the following implications: The probability of no claim is p; the nonnegative claim size X is (with decreasing probability) unlimited above. So the claim size distribution is uniquely characterized by the parameters α and p. If all risks can be described by such a model, the clustering task is to pool those risks with "similar" pairs

$$(p, \alpha)$$

or to identify risks with "similar" expected values

$$E(X) = \int x\,dP_X = \int x\,d(p\delta_0) + \int x\,d((1-p)Exp(\alpha))$$
$$= (1-p)\alpha^{-1}.$$

The penultimate equality holds since we may integrate with respect to the summands of P_X, cf. [Bau92].

As already mentioned, we use a random variable X to model a risk; X typically represents the **annual claim amount** resulting from the associated policy. In our analysis, the following terms shall be important, cf. [Kre99].

Definition 1.3.2 *(i) A **risk** is a family $X := (Y_1, \ldots, Y_t)$ of random variables describing claim amounts $Y_1, \ldots, Y_t$ in successive periods $1, \ldots, t$.*

*(ii) A **collective** is a set $\{X_i \mid i \in \mathbb{N}_n := \{i \in \mathbb{N} \mid i \leq n\}\}$ of risks $(n \in \mathbb{N})$.*

*(iii) A collective is **homogeneous**, if its elements are identically distributed.*

Particularly, (iii) means that the expectations and variances of the random variables X_i are identical.

Presuming the existence of n *independent* risks (which we shall do throughout) $X_1, \ldots, X_n$ and looking at exactly $t = 1$ period, we may specify our probability space as the product

$$(\Omega, \mathcal{A}, P) := \bigotimes_{i=1}^{n} (\mathbb{R}_+, \mathcal{B}_+, P_{X_i}) = \left(\mathbb{R}_+^n, \mathcal{B}_+^n, \bigotimes_{i=1}^{n} P_{X_i} \right)$$

where $\mathbb{R}_+^n := \{x =^t (x_1, \ldots, x_n) \in \mathbb{R}^n \mid x_i \geq 0 \quad (i \in \mathbb{N}_n)\}$ and risk X_i has distribution P_{X_i} $(1 \leq i \leq n)$, $\mathcal{B}_+^n$ is the trace of $\mathcal{B}_n$, the Borel σ-algebra of $\mathbb{R}^n$, in $\mathbb{R}_+^n$. Particularly, this implies

$$P\{X_1 \in B_1, \ldots, X_n \in B_n\} = \prod_{i=1}^{n} P\{X_i \in B_i\}$$

with $B_i \in \mathcal{B}_+$.

The following actuarial terms are substantial for premium pricing purposes, cf. [Hei88] or [BCHJKPR05].

Definition 1.3.3 *(i) The **claim frequency** of a collective in a particular time interval is given by*

$$\frac{number\ of\ claims}{number\ of\ risks} .$$

(ii) *The* **average claim size** *amounts to*

$$\frac{total\ claim\ size}{number\ of\ claims}.$$

(iii) *The* **claims expenditure** *is the ratio*

$$\frac{total\ claim\ size}{number\ of\ risks}.$$

(iv) *The* **claims ratio** *or* **loss ratio** *is given by*

$$\frac{total\ claim\ size}{total\ premium}.$$

Hence,

claims expenditure = claim frequency · average claim size.

For premium pricing purposes, the key figure is the **claims expenditure**. It is the empirical counterpart of the expected claim size of a collective consisting of i.i.d. risks. The calculation of premiums depends heavily upon this quantity. Finally, we define one of the major actuarial terms, cf. [Rad08].

Definition 1.3.4 *Let* $\mathcal{K} := \{X_i \,|\, i \in \mathbb{N}_n\}$ $(n \in \mathbb{N})$ *be a collective, let* C *denote subsets of* $\mathcal{K}$ *and let* $\pi : \mathcal{K} \longrightarrow \mathbb{R}$ *denote monetary amounts. A* **tariff** *is a map* $X_i \mapsto (C(X_i), \pi(X_i))$. *A subset* $C(X_i) \subset \mathcal{K}$ *is referred to as* **tariff class**.

We shall specify the map $\pi : \mathcal{K} \longrightarrow \mathbb{R}$ in definition 2.1.1 and then refer to the monetary amounts $\pi(X_i)$ as to *premiums*. In definition 1.3.4, a risk X_i is normally characterized by the corresponding levels of rating variables and its individual claim experience in order to assign an adequate premium.

1.4 A Plan of this Investigation

The superordinate target of our analysis is appropriately calculating (non-life) insurance premiums. Thus we state some fundamentals of premium pricing in **Chapter 2**. Besides some general remarks and the discussion of models for computing the total claim size of an insurance collective, we are particularly concerned with credibility theory, a very powerful and sophisticated tool in insurance mathematics designed for an optimal calculation of premiums. Credibility arguments turn out to be a key idea for our classification algorithm to be developed later on.

Our – somewhat technical – **Chapter 3** highlights the statistical and geometrical basis of cluster analysis, which is the multivariate statistical procedure eligible for classifying data sets into homogeneous categories. From a mathematical viewpoint, the user typically needs an algorithm to solve a clustering problem. In general, the application of heuristic algorithms does not guarantee to reach an absolute optimum of the target function, the cluster criterion. In contrast, a quadratic optimization model proposed by [BG04] has the capability to find an absolute optimum of such target functions.

Within this chapter, we also discuss which aspects have to be taken into account when classifying an insurance collective. Tariff variables have to be identified in the first place. An important condition is to ensure the balance of the subcollectives (tariff classes); in this context, we look at the determination of cluster cardinalities. Additionally, one has to ask of which *length* the partition of a data set ought to be; in our application, this means assessing the number of tariff classes.

Chapter 4 is an inventory taking of classification methods in non-life insurance mathematics. *Cross classification (CC)* schemes doubtlessly offer a variety of desirable features which we shall discuss. Moreover, we look at the concrete design of CC and concepts for premium pricing within this framework. Basically, CC schemes generate specification classes of each tariff variable; the resulting partition of an insurance collective thus has a matrix structure (yielding tariff *cells*). This matrix structure – though it divides the collective into easily distinguishable subsets – involves problems to be discussed (in the next chapter). Essentially, clustering tasks are *one*dimensional within the CC framework. To illustrate the latter item, we bring a prominent example from car insurance, namely the generation of territory classes.

Based on our results gained in the course of the investigation up to Chapter 4, we record some weak points of CC systems and put forward a new algorithm, the *multidimensional credibility-based classification algorithm (MC)* in **Chapter 5**. First of all, MC adopts the advantages of CC. The construction of MC is based on two aspects: First, MC makes use of credibility theory. Second, the clustering task is carried out not one-dimensionally but in higher dimension. They key to understand the effectiveness of MC is the *measurement of the distance between two risks*. We prove the most important theoretical statements concerning MC, particularly its relationship to CC. More precisely, under certain assumptions, CC turns out to be a special case of MC. Thus we have found a more general method to classify an insurance collective than those methods being currently used.

A characteristic feature of MC is to interchange pricing and classifying: Normally, credibility theory is used at the final pricing stage of premium calculation; here, we make use of credibility already in the classification stage of premium calculation. As a sort of "byproduct" serves our interpretation of the (fixed) credibility factor as an indicator of how close the "natural" structure of the collective (the atomic cells) comes to fulfil the conditions of the laws of large numbers. Note therefore that the credibility factor is defined to be some real number between 0 and 1.

Having worked out the theoretical benefits of MC, we turn to its empirical investigation in **Chapter 6** by means of a prognostive test and associated familiar criteria related to actuarial balance and goodness of fit. CC serves as a benchmark for measuring the performance of MC. In five out of six criteria, we find that MC outperforms CC, confirming the desirable theoretical properties derived in the previous chapter. A brief outlook formulates further topics to be discussed in the context of MC and concludes our analysis.

Finally, the **Appendix** contains all data necessary for the empirical analysis in Chapter 6, i.e. information concerning the structure of the used collective and claims data.

Chapter 2

Fundamentals of Premium Pricing

2.1 General Remarks

For the course of our considerations, it makes sense to review briefly the **levels of tariff calculation** now, see e.g. [vEGN83]. Usually, there are three subsequent steps in the ratemaking procedure:

1. Selection of tariff variables

2. Determination of tariff classes

3. Calculation of the expected claims expenditure (for each tariff class).

As far as this investigation is concerned, we shall mainly discuss task 2. Task 1 is covered in Section 3.5.2 when we discuss some selected problems from cluster analysis applied to applications in insurance, namely the choice of rating variables. Task 3 is the final step of ratemaking; Section 4.2 deals with the most commonly used methods to compute the rate for tariff cells in a cross-classified collective.

2.1.1 Objectives and Techniques of Premium Pricing

We now discuss major objectives of premium rating, namely (a) regulatory considerations and (b) business considerations, see [Rej03] or [WSY98].

(a) *Regulatory objectives* e.g. in the U.S. require premiums to be adequate (i.e. high enough to cover losses and expenses), not excessive (i.e. premiums must not provide excessive profits to the insurer) and not unfairly discriminatory (i.e. exposures representing a similar level of riskiness should be charged the same rate and premiums ought to reflect the amount of risk accurately). As far as German regulations regarding car insurance are concerned, legal foundations are Section 11 VAG[1] and the TVO[2]. [Sie88] and [Hel78] summarize the most important aspects: (i) similar risks have to be grouped into risk classes, (ii) premiums *must* be differentiated according to objective risk factors, (iii) premiums *may* be differentiated according to subjective risks factors, if these can be clearly determined, if the formed groups allow for the group balance concept and if their claims expenditure differs significantly from the overall claims expenditure of the entire portfolio.

(b) *Business objectives* require premium rating to be simple and understandable, so that rate making is inexpensive to apply. Also should premiums be stable in the short run, as frequently varying premiums irritate policy holders. In the long run however, rates should be responsive to economic changes and changing loss exposures. Finally, premiums should encourage loss control activities as such activities

---

[1]Versicherungsaufsichtsgesetz
[2]Verordnung über die Tarife in der Kraftfahrzeug-Haftpflichtversicherung

can help to avoid claims. For instance, installing a car alarm device may be able to prevent car theft and should be rebated.

Summarizing up, from the insurers' perspective this means first, that a contract (policy) has to be priced in a manner that the premiums are sufficient to settle payments arising from possible claims and second, that premiums are not too high as the policy holders may exercise their right to choose their insurer. Premium pricing must be carried out within this framework of neither too low nor too high premiums. The goal is thus to set **risk adequate** premiums for each customer.

We shall now briefly introduce the three principal rating procedures to motivate the need for classification methods in non-life insurance. They are (a) individual or judgment rating, (b) class or manual rating and (c) merit or modification rating, see [Rej03] and [WSY98].

(a) *Judgment* or *individual rating* means that the premium is set by the underwriter's judgment and each exposure is to be evaluated individually. Therefore, each policyholder is charged an individual premium. This method is applied to the insurance of ocean-going vessels and their cargoes, or to pieces of art, or technical innovations for instance. Generally speaking, individual rating is used for insuring unusual exposures. These exposures are often so diverse that a class rate (see below) cannot be calculated. A prominent example is the insurance of the LHC (Large Hadron Collider) operated by CERN (Conseil Européen pour la Recherche Nucléaire), cf. [GDV08d]. In such cases, present practice divides the total risk into several components and checks whether some of these parts are already known. Credible claims statistics for such exposures are often not available (though they would be necessary to calculate class rates). Clearly, important shortcomings of this method are its reliance on human judgment as the sole consideration and its time consuming rating process

34

which does not meet the above mentioned business objectives very well.[3] Important aspects when underwriting such policies are high participations and risk sharing among insurer and reinsurer.

(b) *Class* or *manual rating* is the most widely used method to set insurance premiums. This method groups exposures into various – with respect to some characteristics, the so called tariff variables – homogeneous classes, and each policyholder belonging to the same class is charged the same rate. Class rating is based upon the assumption that the insureds' future losses depend upon a certain set of factors. For instance, the following characteristics (among others) are commonly used in automobile liability insurance: age of policyholder, gender, marital status, driving record, address of policyholder, use of the vehicle of the insured, no-claims discount (NCD) level[4], vehicle age and vehicle model. These factors are assumed to affect the likelihood and severity of a claim. The term manual rating stems from the publication of the class rates in a rating manual which is used to determine the premium for a particular policyholder.

(c) *Merit* or *modification rating* is a kind of adjustment of class premiums. This adjustment occurs according to the prior loss experience of an exposure: Class rates are modified to reflect his or her past individual loss experience. Basically, conclusions drawn from the past loss experience are to serve as a basis to make predictions regarding expected losses in the future. There are several types of modification rating:

- Applying *schedule rating*, each exposure is initially assigned a basis rate which is then modified by debits or credits for undesirable or desirable characteristics of the exposure. In practice, a comparison of some

---

[3]More articulately, [Wit86] considers premium pricing for satellite insurance contracts "guesswork".
[4]In fact, this is a form of modification rating.

specified features is carried out between a standard insured and the insured who is to be rated. These characteristics are assumed to influence the insured's future claim sizes. Schedule rating is principally applied to the pricing of premiums in fire insurance.

- *Experience rating* includes the insured's past loss experience to set the premium. In practice, a formerly determined class rate is adjusted according to the loss experience of typically the past three years to calculate the premium for the next policy year. Normally, the experience rating method is limited to large organizations e.g. in general liability insurance.

- Using *retrospective rating*, the actual premium depends on the insured's loss experience in the current period. This means that, at the beginning of the policy period, a provisional rate has to be paid. The final premium is calculated at the end of that period, taking the occurred losses during this period into account. Of course, there exist a minimum and a maximum premium to be paid. This form of rate making is used in glass or car insurance, for instance.

- *Premium discounts* can be awarded to insureds paying large premiums. A typical example is the insurance of vehicle fleets, if 5, say, or more vehicles under one ownership are to be insured.

Let us make the following convention, see [AL88]: By the term *premium*, we mean the *pure premium* (or *risk premium* or *net premium*) throughout this text. The pure premium is the *net risk premium* (the expected loss resulting from a contract) plus a *safety loading*, and by considering the pure premium we refer to that portion of the gross premium that is necessary to cover/pay out the losses. The other components of the gross premium besides the pure premium – loadings for expenses, discounts for investment income and profit loadings – do not pose new actuarial problems and will thus not be considered further.

The principal actuarial task is calculating premiums. In non-life insurance mathematics, it is customary for this purpose to make use of premium principles, see [Sch06] and [GVH84]. In the following definition, P_X denotes the *distribution* of the random variable X under P.

Definition 2.1.1 *A* **premium principle** *is a map*

$$\pi : \mathcal{R} := \{X \mid X \text{ is a risk}\} \longrightarrow \mathbb{R}, \quad X \mapsto \pi(X)$$

such that the following conditions hold:
$\forall X, Y \in \mathcal{R}$

(i) $P_X = P_Y \Longrightarrow \pi(X) = \pi(Y)$

(ii) $E(X) \leq \pi(X)$

(iii) $P\{X > \pi(X)\} > 0.$

Condition (i) requires that risks with the same degree of riskiness (the same distribution) is charged the same premium. According to (ii), the premium is not less than the expected loss. Finally, property (iii) is a no-arbitrage condition.

Some desirable properties of premium calculation principles are particularly the following, see [KGDD01] and [Hei87]:

(a) *Translation invariance*, occasionally referred to as *consistency*:

$$\forall c \in \mathbb{R} \quad \forall X \in \mathcal{R} : \quad \pi(X + c) = \pi(X) + c.$$

A risk exceeding (or undercutting) a given risk X by the constant amount c should be priced higher (or lower) by that quantity.

(b) *Homogeneity*:

$$\forall c \in \mathbb{R} \quad \forall X \in \mathcal{R} : \quad \pi(cX) = c\pi(X).$$

This requirement is plausible in terms of coinsurance or converting risks and premiums into a different currency.

(c) *No unjustified fluctuation loading:*

$$X = c \quad P - a.s. \quad \Longrightarrow \quad \pi(X) = c$$

$(c \in \mathbb{R})$.

(d) *Additivity:*

$$X, Y \in \mathcal{R} \quad \text{independent} \quad \Longrightarrow \quad \pi(X+Y) = \pi(X) + \pi(Y).$$

If independent risks are cumulated, the total premium of these risks together should equal the single premiums.[5]

(e) π should be *bounded* by the maximum compensation: Hence,

$$\pi(X) \leq F^{-1}(1)$$

for all $X \in \mathcal{R}$; the distribution function of X is denoted by F.

(f) In case there exists a relation (an order) $\prec$ on $\mathcal{R}$, and this relation can be interpreted in a suitable manner, it makes sense to call for the following condition:

$$X \prec Y \quad \Longrightarrow \quad \pi(X) \leq \pi(Y).$$

Examples of $\prec$ on $\mathcal{R}$ are the *stochastic order* and the *stop-loss order*, see [Sch06].

(g) Occasionally, premium principles are required to be *convex*:[6]

$$\pi(pX + (1-p)Y) \leq p\pi(X) + (1-p)\pi(Y) \quad (X, Y \in \mathcal{R};$$
$$p \in]0, 1[).$$

Convexity can ease the analysis of certain problems: [DG85] solve two problems using convex premium principles, namely

---

[5]Instead of additivity, occasionally *subadditivity* $(\pi(X+Y) \leq \pi(X) + \pi(Y))$ or *superadditivity* $(\pi(X+Y) \geq \pi(X) + \pi(Y))$, respectively, are desired. Justifications for each type of additivity are given in [Hei87].

[6]This property generalizes definition 2.1.1 insofar as risks having the same distributions do not necessarily lead to the same premium.

(i) an optimal purchase of reinsurance, i.e. what degree of reinsurance should be chosen and (ii) an optimal form of cooperation, i.e. how can several insurance firms split up a given risk in order to minimize the total premium.[7]

Next, let us consider briefly some of the most important premium principles, see [GVH84]. Roughly speaking, there are two sorts: Pragmatic (like the expected value principle) and more theoretical (like the zero utility principle) premium calculation principles. It is well-known that the following examples are indeed premium principles in the sense of definition 2.1.1.

Examples 2.1.2   (a) The fundamental approach is the *equivalence principle* or *net premium principle*, stating

$$\pi(X) = E(X).$$

(b) The *expected value principle* includes a proportional (to the expected value of X) loading $\alpha E(X)$:

$$\pi(X) = (1 + \alpha)E(X)$$

where $\alpha > 0$.

(c) Moreover, the *variance principle* takes the variance of the tarified risk into account:

$$\pi(X) = E(X) + \alpha V(X)$$

for $\alpha > 0$.

(d) Likewise, the *standard deviation principle* is defined by

$$\pi(X) = E(X) + \alpha \sigma_X$$

for $\alpha > 0$. Here, quantities having the same dimension are added. Moreover, [Alb84a] shows that the standard deviation principle is to be preferred in terms of the group balance concept (measured by the one periodic ruin probability) against the variance principle.

---

[7]A decomposition of a risk X (into two parts) can be formulated as $X = pX + (1 - p)X$ $(p \in]0, 1[)$.

(e) To apply the *percentile principle*, one has to know the distribution function F of the claim size X, hence this approach is principally of theoretical importance:

$$\pi(X) = \inf\{x \mid F(x) \geq 1 - \varepsilon\}$$

for $\varepsilon \in]0, 1[$. Application of this principle ensures that the probability of a payout (from the insurer's perspective) is at most ε. In case the distribution function F is invertible, we may rewrite this principle as

$$\pi(X) = F^{-1}(1 - \varepsilon).$$

(f) The *principle of zero utility* requires a utility function[8] u and is the solution to the equation

$$u(0) = E\left(u(\pi(X) - X)\right).$$

Choosing $u := \mathrm{id}$, i.e. $u(x) = x$, the net premium principle results. One can interprete $u(0)$ and $u(\pi(X) - X)$ to be the utility of the present capital and the utility of the capital after having insured risk X for premium $\pi(X)$, respectively. According to this rationale, the rate should be set in a way such that the expected utility equals the zero utility.

(g) The *Esscher principle* assigns the rate

$$\pi(X) = \frac{E(Xe^{\alpha X})}{E(e^{\alpha X})}$$

for $\alpha > 0$ to risk X.

[Hei87] provides an overview which premium principles satisfy which desirable properties as stated above.

Remember our discussion of differentiating premiums in Chapter 1. When using the standard deviation principle, the following surprising effect observed by [Alb84a] occurs. It reveals a

---

[8] A utility function u assigns a real number $u(x)$ to a monetary amount x and is strictly monotonic increasing and concave.

circumstance which suggests *not* to cluster an insurance collective at first glance but to ask all policyholders for the same premium.

Example 2.1.3 Suppose we are given a heterogeneous collective $\mathcal{K}$ of $n := |\mathcal{K}|$ independent risks and total claim size S and use the standard deviation principle (see example 2.1.2 below) in order to set premiums. We wish to compare the following two situations in terms of premium pricing:

(a) each risk in our collective is assigned a common premium

(b) suppose a homogeneous (in terms of expectations and variances of the claim sizes) subdivision $\{C_1, \ldots, C_k\}$ of $\mathcal{K}$ has been found and each risk class C_i $(1 \leq i \leq k)$ is assigned its risk adequate rate.[9]

Further, we set the same ruin probability in either case. This choice of the ruin probability determines the value of the parameter α in 2.1.2: Having fixed some ruin probability, α is to be controlled either by Cantelli's inequality (proposition 3.5.7) or by the central limit theorem. As for the standard deviation principle, the value of α is then particularly independent from the collective size. This is a special property of the standard deviation principle which has been shown by [Alb84a]. Hence we shall use the same value of α below to analyze situations (a) and (b). Writing κ_i for the size of C_i and thus $n = \sum_{i=1}^{k} \kappa_i$, further writing S_i for the total claim size of C_i and thus $S = \sum_{i=1}^{k} S_i$ for the claim size of $\mathcal{K}$, and μ_i and $\sigma_i \neq 0$ for the (common) expected claim size and variance, respectively, for the risks belonging to C_i, we have

$$E(S_i) = \kappa_i \mu_i, \quad \sigma(S_i) = \sqrt{\kappa_i} \sigma_i, \quad E(S) = \sum_{i=1}^{k} \kappa_i \mu_i,$$

$$\sigma(S) = \sqrt{\sum_{i=1}^{k} \kappa_i \sigma_i^2}.$$

---

[9]In either situation, we refer to the respective *collective* premium(s).

In situation (b), the premium for C_i amounts to

$$\pi(S_i) = \kappa_i \mu_i + \alpha \sqrt{\kappa_i} \sigma_i$$

and the total premium for $\mathcal{K}$ is thus

$$\pi_{(b)}(S) = \sum_{i=1}^{k} \pi(S_i) = \sum_{i=1}^{k} \kappa_i \mu_i + \alpha \sum_{i=1}^{k} \sqrt{\kappa_i} \sigma_i. \qquad (2.1)$$

In situation (a), the total premium for $\mathcal{K}$ is

$$\pi_{(a)}(S) = \sum_{i=1}^{k} \kappa_i \mu_i + \alpha \sqrt{\sum_{i=1}^{k} \kappa_i \sigma_i^2}. \qquad (2.2)$$

Now we pose the question when it is cheaper to behave according to (a), i.e. not to cluster. Obviously, we have to compare (2.2) and (2.1): The condition for preferring (a) is $\pi_{(a)}(S) < \pi_{(b)}(S)$, i.e.

$$\sqrt{\sum_{i=1}^{k} \kappa_i \sigma_i^2} < \sum_{i=1}^{k} \sqrt{\kappa_i} \sigma_i$$

which is always fulfilled since $\|a\|_2 < \|a\|_1$ for $\mathbb{R}^k \ni a :=^t (a_1, \ldots, a_k) \neq 0$ (choose $a_i := \sqrt{\kappa_i} \sigma_i \quad (1 \leq i \leq k)$).

Hence (a) leads to a collective premium for $\mathcal{K}$ which is always below the collective premium (sum of all premiums of the subclasses) as calculated in situation (b). Under our assumptions, it is thus always cheaper to combine heterogeneous risks rather than to install a risk classification scheme and grade premiums according to the perceived riskiness. $\qquad \square$

However, this result has to be interpreted very carefully. Since insurance markets are highly competitive and in order to come up against the adverse selection problem, it is nevertheless necessary to risk-adjust premiums rather than to pool heterogeneous risks although this yields a higher collective premium. Moreover, the assumption of equal ruin probabilities needs not necessarily be fulfilled if α is to be controlled by the central limit theorem. Since we deal with a *heterogeneous* collective, the application of the central limit theorem is not obvious – particularly, its classical version presumes a sequence of i.i.d. random variables.

2.1.2 Determinants of Preferable Classification Systems

In the insurance business, it is customary to implement risk classification schemes, particularly in such cases where sufficient claim experience for an individual risk is not available in order to derive a price, see [Fin04]. Similar risks (with respect to expected claim cost) are then grouped together, and the same premium is assigned to all members belonging to the same group. Let us briefly outline attributes which determine the quality of risk classification systems, see [Fel04]:

(a) *Equity*: Premiums ought to mirror expected claim cost.

(b) *Homogeneity*: There should be no subgroups within a particular risk class, such that these subgroups have different expected claim cost.

(c) *Intuition*: The classification variables should be intuitively related to the loss hazards.

(d) *Practicality*: Rating variables should be objective in the sense of being clearly measurable, such that the insured cannot manipulate their values.

(e) *Incentives*: If possible, the classification system should provide incentives to a risk-reducing behaviour.

(f) *Legal*: Legal regulations apply.

We give an example of how these aspects may affect the selection of tariff variables: Due to (c) and (f) it would be critical to consider characteristics such as "sex" or "race" suitable predictor variables. Nevertheless, some states do use such attributes in their rating process.

Before turning to applications of cluster techniques in risk management of insurance firms, let us outline some aspects of classification schemes which are generally important, see [HH97]:

(a) classification accuracy (there should be no misclassified objects)

(b) speed of classification (an instant rating is preferable)

(c) ease of understanding (why and how has the scheme come to its conclusion?).

2.2 Loss Models

Not only for pricing purposes an insurer has to develop an aggregate loss model. The aggregate loss of the insurer is the total sum of claims in a certain period (usually one year) and is denoted by S. There are two major approaches, the individual and collective model, to determine the distribution of S, both of which we shall describe briefly, see e.g. [NRR95] or [Ger79].

2.2.1 The Individual Model

Definition 2.2.1 *Let X_i $(i \in \mathbb{N}_n)$ be risks. The family $(X_i)_{i \in \{1,...,n\}}$ is an **individual model**, if it is independent.*

The total claim (e.g. in one year) in the individual model is determined by the sum of the claims of all risks

$$S := \sum_{i=1}^{n} X_i,$$

i.e. by the sum of the claims of all risks (n is the size of the collective). Based upon assumptions regarding the distributions

P_{X_i} of the risks X_i, one can compute the distribution of S. Generally, the distribution of S is given by the convolution

$$P_S = P_{X_1} * \cdots * P_{X_n}.$$

In many situations one is mainly concerned with certain moments of the loss distribution like its expectation and variance.[10] In case of a homogeneous collective of size n and with total loss S, and $E(X_i) =: \mu_i =: \mu$ and $V(X_i) =: \sigma_i^2 =: \sigma^2$ $(1 \leq i \leq n)$ it follows by the linearity of the expectation and the equality of Bienaymé, respectively, that

$$E(S) = n\mu$$

and

$$V(S) = n\sigma^2.$$

However, in case of a heterogeneous portfolio, the total loss S is then modelled as $S = \sum_{i=1}^{n} D_i X_i$, see [INZ05] or [Ger79]. In this expression, the D_i's are random variables indicating whether or not the ith risk causes a payment: $D_i = 1$ iff policy i produces exactly one payment and $D_i = 0$ iff there is no claim (during the considered period of time). Further, we set $p_i := P\{D_i = 1\}$ and $P\{D_i = 0\} := 1 - p_i$, this means particularly that the case of two or more claims per policy is excluded.[11] The X_i's represent the amount of the claim by policy i given that a loss occurred (i.e. given that $D_i = 1$). The $2n$ random variables $D_1, \ldots, D_n, X_1, \ldots, X_n$ are assumed to be independent. We give expressions for the expectation and variance of the collective claim size S calculated according to the individual model.

Proposition 2.2.2 *The expected collective claim size is given by*

$$E(S) = \sum_{i=1}^{n} p_i E(X_i)$$

---

[10] As we have seen, various premium principles depend solely upon the first two moments of the corresponding risk.

[11] [Lem85] considers 9,996 claiming policy holders. It turns out that 756 (approximately 7.6%) of them cause two or more accidents per year. It is also found that the average claim cost of drivers with three or four claims is significantly less than that for drivers with only one or two accidents.

and its variance by

$$V(S) = \sum_{i=1}^{n} \left(p_i V(X_i) + p_i(1 - p_i) \left[E(X_i)\right]^2 \right).$$

Proof. We can express the total claim size by $S = \sum_{i=1}^{n} D_i X_i$, hence it follows:

(i) As for the expectation, this yields

$$
\begin{aligned}
E(S) &= \sum_{i=1}^{n} E(D_i X_i) \\
&= \sum_{i=1}^{n} E(D_i) E(X_i) \\
&= \sum_{i=1}^{n} p_i E(X_i)
\end{aligned}
$$

since for independent random variables D_i, X_i the identity $E(D_i X_i) = E(D_i)E(X_i)$ holds and obviously $E(D_i) = p_i$ (the D_i's have Bernoulli-distributions).

(ii) Computing the variance yields

$$
\begin{aligned}
V(S) &= \sum_{i=1}^{n} V(D_i X_i) \\
&= \sum_{i=1}^{n} \left(E\left([D_i X_i]^2\right) - [E(D_i X_i)]^2 \right) \\
&= \sum_{i=1}^{n} \left(E(D_i^2) E(X_i^2) - [E(D_i X_i)]^2 \right) \\
&= \sum_{i=1}^{n} \left(p_i E(X_i^2) - p_i^2 \left[E(X_i)\right]^2 \right) \\
&= \sum_{i=1}^{n} \left(p_i V(X_i) + p_i(1 - p_i) \left[E(X_i)\right]^2 \right).
\end{aligned}
$$

Now clustering techniques may be used to form homogeneous (in terms of profitability and volatility) subcollectives (risk groups) of the whole insurance portfolio. Having found these risk groups, the distribution of the total claim size for each risk class can be determined; it is assumed that all risks belonging to the same risk category have the same distribution function.[12] [Mac02] suggests using (i) the gamma distribution or (ii) the inverse Gaussian distribution to model the claim size distributions of the risks X_i.

The individual model has certain shortcomings. Clearly, the assumption of concrete individual distribution functions is problematic: How can one obtain the required distribution functions of the risks? In terms of computational techniques, another problem is the lavishness of calculating the corresponding convolution for large n.

2.2.2 The Collective Model

We now introduce the collective model for the collective claim size.

Definition 2.2.3 *Let N be a random variable on $(\Omega, \mathcal{A}, P)$ taking values in $\mathbb{N}_0$ and let X_i $(i \in \mathbb{N})$ be claim amounts. The pair $(N, (X_i)_{i \in \mathbb{N}})$ is a **collective model**, if the X_i are i.i.d. and independent from N.*

The total claim size S in a given period of time is given by the sum of the claims X_i $(i = 1, \ldots, N)$, hence by

$$S := \sum_{i=1}^{N} X_i$$

---

[12] According to the central limit theorem, the distribution of the standardized collective claim size tends toward a normal distribution for i.i.d. risks, but how many risks justify assuming normality?

(with the convention $\{S = 0\}$ if $\{N = 0\}$). On using the multiplication theorem for probabilities, the law of total probability and independence, the distribution function of S is given by

$$F_S(x) := P\left\{\sum_{i=1}^{N} X_i \leq x\right\} = \sum_{n=0}^{\infty} P\{N = n\} F^{n*}(x),$$

see e.g. [KGDD01]. Obviously, F_S depends upon the distribution of N and the distribution of the X_i's (the latter are i.i.d. and independent from N by definition). In view of the i.i.d.-condition we may write X for the typical claim size.

As already mentioned, it is sufficient in various situations to have expressions for the first two moments of the distribution of S. Hence we give expressions for its expectation and variance. These identitites are commonly referred to as *Wald equations*.

Proposition 2.2.4 *The expectation and variance of the collective claim size are given by*

$$E(S) = E(N)E(X)$$

and

$$V(S) = E(N)V(X) + V(N)\left(E(X)\right)^2,$$

respectively.

Proof. See [Ger79]. □

To model the distribution of the number of claims in a given period of time, it is customary to use the Poisson distribution, the binomial distribution or the negative binomial distribution, see [NRR95].

To model the distribution of the claim amounts, the lognormal distribution, the log-Laplace distribution and the Weibull distribution are commonly used, see [Str88] or [Mac02]. The parameter(s) of all mentioned probability laws can be estimated by the usual estimation techniques, e.g. by the maximum-likelihood method, by least squares or by the methods of moments from past claims data, see [Mac02].

The collective model has turned out to be a very powerful tool to deal with the randomness of the total loss. Comparing it to the individual model, it has several advantages, see [Mac02] and [Sch06]:

(a) It is meaningless whether or not the portfolio is homogeneous.

(b) The i.i.d.-assumption for the single claims is more realistic than it is for the total claim sizes per risk.

(c) The claim count distribution (i.e. the distribution of N) and the distribution (there is only one) of the claim sizes (we may write X to denote the typical claim size) can be estimated reliably, particularly more reliably than the claim size distributions of the homogeneous risk groups in the individual model. In fact, this is a major reason for the superiority of the collective model. The statistical basis is wider than that one of an individual model as the parameters of solely exactly two distributions have to be estimated. Assuming individual models for the homogeneous risk groups, there are as many distributions as risk collectives.

(d) Having techniques to assess the distribution P_S of the total loss S in view, the collective model is computationally more efficient: Though there are more convolutions to be carried out, due to recursion formulae and today's capable computers this can be coped with.

Depending on the particular situation, one has to pose the question which of the two models is appropriate. Here, we are mainly concerned with premium pricing. Though we have highlighted some desirable characteristics of the collective model, the individual model is more important in the framework of our analysis: The latter is necessary to model moments – particularly the expectations and the variances – of the collective claim sizes of several risk groups (subsets of a given collective). These figures

49

are the basis of premium calculation. So the structure of a tariff system itself is determined mainly by the individual model – this premium pricing aspect is the major issue of our considerations. By contrast, the collective model is used to derive statements regarding insurance campanies' safety levels and equity requirements in the first instance, as well as the demand for reinsurance, cf. [Mac02]. In order to compute the safety level of a company, it is particularly important to assess the tail of the claim size distribution; this task can be solved more reliably by using the collective model.

In the case of i.i.d. X_i $(1 \leq i \leq n)$, the individual model turns out to be a special case of the collective model, namely that one with $\{N = n\}$ P-a.s., cf. [KPW04].

2.3 Optimal Estimation and Credibility Theory

In the past few decades, credibility theory has become a very popular part of actuarial mathematics. Here, we review a certain aspect given attention to in credibility theory. In order to understand the motivation of our new classification system being proposed later on, we shall present the key ideas of credibility theory very briefly. References are [vSc89] and [KGDD01], for instance. A brief introduction to credibility models applied to practical car insurance problems provides [HK01]; [Rau98] is devoted to applications in industrial fire insurance.

Originally, the term *credibility* was used to refer to the claims experience of a particular risk in time, i.e. the risk is considered over several periods $1, \ldots, t$, and the goal was to take this individual claim information into account when setting the premium for that risk. The underlying idea is that each risk should pay its own claim cost in the long run, see [DPP94]. However, another interpretation is possible (note that we have only one time period in our empirical examination later on), so we are going to approach the problem of questionable claims information from a slightly different angle:

Suppose we are given a collective $\mathcal{K}$. Credibility models determine the premium π_C (for the next period) of a group of risks $C \subset \mathcal{K}$ as a convex combination of two claims expenditures, more precisely the premium is calculated according to

$$\pi_C = \gamma_C x_C + (1 - \gamma_C) E(X_\mathcal{K}) \qquad (2.3)$$

where $E(X_\mathcal{K})$ denotes the expected claims expenditure of the entire collective $\mathcal{K}$ (or some other "meaningful" superset of C) and x_C is the claims expenditure of risk class C; $0 \leq \gamma_C \leq 1$ is referred to as *credibility factor*. It expresses how "credible" the group's claims expenditure is; a premium calculated according to this formula is referred to as *credibility premium* or *credibility estimator*. Of course, it is plausible to obtain a credibility factor close to 1 if the corresponding exposure (number of risks) n is vast (formally: $\gamma_C \longrightarrow 1$ for $n \longrightarrow \infty$) and/or if this exposure shows a stable claims expenditure over time. Formulae of the form (2.3) trace back to the year 1918 where the first seminal paper on credibility theoretical ideas ([Whi18]) appeared. The task of credibility models is to determine "optimal" credibility factors. The most prominent examples of credibility factors are the Bühlmann-estimator (see [Bue67]), the Bühlmann-Straub-estimator (see [BS70]) and the credibility estimator in the framework of hierarchical models proposed by Jewell.

In the next two subsections, we look at two classes of credibility models.

2.3.1 Limited Fluctuation Theory

We give a simple example of a credibility factor as mentioned in [HK01].[13] Therefore, it is necessary to define the *minimum*

---

[13]Basically, [Hel78] considers the same problem when examining the necessary number of risks for keeping the fluctuation of territorial claims expenditures within certain bounds.

number of risks ensuring credibility first. Assume there are enough risks in a collective – against the background of our considerations in Chapter 6 we think of such a collective as an atomic cell – to assume a normally distributed claims expenditure. The normality assumption is justified by the central limit theorem when we presume that the risks in the collective are i.i.d., which should be fulfilled as there are only homogeneous risks in the collective producing their claims independently from another. By the i.i.d-property of the risks, we write X_i $(i = 1, \ldots, \kappa_C)$ for their claim sizes, n for the size of the collective and $E(X_i) =: E(X) =: \mu$ and $V(X_i) =: V(X) =: \sigma^2 > 0$. Note that the counterpart of μ (stochastic level) is the claims expenditure $X_C := \frac{\sum_{i=1}^{n} X_i}{\kappa_C}$ (empirical level) with realization x_C. Consequently, we expect C to have claims expenditure μ. Now we can ask how many risks κ^* are necessary such that at most $100\alpha\%$ of them have claim sizes deviating from μ by more than $\varepsilon > 0$, i.e.

$$P\{|X_C - \mu| \geq \varepsilon\} \leq \alpha. \qquad (2.4)$$

From the sample $X_1, \ldots, X_{\kappa_C}$ and by the central limit theorem we obtain that $\frac{X_C - \mu}{\sigma}\sqrt{\kappa_C}$ is approximately standard normally distributed. On rearranging, (2.4) yields

$$P\{|X_C - \mu| < \varepsilon\} \qquad \geq 1 - \alpha$$
$$\Leftrightarrow \qquad P\{X_C - \mu < \varepsilon\} \qquad \geq 1 - \frac{\alpha}{2}$$
$$\Leftrightarrow \quad P\left\{(X_C - \mu)\frac{\sqrt{\kappa_C}}{\sigma} < \frac{\varepsilon\sqrt{\kappa_C}}{\sigma}\right\} \quad \geq 1 - \frac{\alpha}{2}$$
$$\Leftrightarrow \qquad \frac{\varepsilon\sqrt{\kappa_C}}{\sigma} \qquad \geq u_{1-\frac{\alpha}{2}}$$
$$\Leftrightarrow \qquad \kappa_C \qquad \geq \frac{u_{1-\frac{\alpha}{2}}^2 \sigma^2}{\varepsilon^2} =: \kappa^*, \quad (2.5)$$

where $u_{1-\frac{\alpha}{2}}$ is the $(1 - \frac{\alpha}{2})$-quantile of the standard normal distribution. So if the number of risks is higher than κ^*, the probability that the future observed claims expenditure x deviates from μ by less than ε is at least $1 - \alpha$. If the size of a collective C is κ^* (or even more), C is said to have *full credibility*. If C contains less than κ^* risks, C is said to have *partial credibility*.

The following example provides a suggestion for a credibility factor for a collective C of size $\kappa_C < \kappa^*$ and minimum number of risks κ^*.

Example 2.3.1 Occasionally, the formula

$$\gamma_C := \min\left\{\sqrt{\frac{\kappa_C}{\kappa^*}}, 1\right\}. \qquad (2.6)$$

is used to assess partial credibility, see e.g. [Nor79]. Since $\sqrt{x} \geq x$ for $x \in [0,1]$, the credibility of a collective with size less than κ^* is higher than the ratio $\frac{\kappa_C}{\kappa^*}$, e.g. a collective having only 25% of the minimum number of risks yet has credibility 50%. A premium, calculated by means of this credibility factor, is referred to as *limited fluctuation credibility formula*. A justification for formula (2.6) is the following consideration: If the premium for the next period is fixed according to (2.3), the error

$$\pi_C - \mu = \gamma_C(X_C - \mu) + (1 - \gamma_C)(X_\mathcal{K} - \mu)$$

(that is the difference between charged premium π_C and actual expected claim size μ) comes up. The first summand is due to an error in the estimate of the individual claim experience X_C of C and the second one is due to misspecification of the overall claims expenditure $X_\mathcal{K}$. Now if we require the first summand being absolutely bounded by $p\mu$ with some $p > 0$ and probability not less than $1 - \alpha$, formally:

$$P\{\gamma_C|X_C - \mu| \leq p\mu\} \geq 1 - \alpha,$$

then

$$\gamma_C \leq \sqrt{\frac{\kappa_C}{\kappa^*}}$$

must hold: Similar to our computations above, one obtains

$$\kappa_C \geq \frac{u_{1-\frac{\alpha}{2}}^2 \sigma^2 \gamma_C^2}{\varepsilon^2} = \kappa^* \gamma_C^2$$

and thus the claim. $\qquad\qquad\qquad\qquad\qquad\qquad\qquad\square$

The next example shows for concrete values of the relevant parameters how a credibility premium can be computed.

Example 2.3.2 Practitioners usually assert concrete values for μ (and σ^2) and express the deviation ε of X from μ in terms of μ. Typically, one sets $\varepsilon := p\mu$ for some $p > 0$. Let us consider collective C consisting of $n = 5,000$ risks with $\mu = 200$ [Euro] and $\sigma = 1,000$ [Euro]. Further, we select a maximum deviation of 10%, i.e. $p = 0.1$ and confidence level 95%. Formula (3.5.3) yields $\kappa^* \approx \left(\frac{1.96 \cdot 1,000}{0.1 \cdot 200}\right)^2 = 9,604$. Thus C has credibility $\gamma_C \approx \sqrt{\frac{5,000}{9,604}} \approx 0.7215$. If $C \subset \mathcal{K}$ and $\mathcal{K}$ has claims expenditure 300 [Euro], its premium amounts to $\pi_C \approx 0.7215 \cdot 200 + (1 - 0.7215) \cdot 300 \approx 227.85$ [Euro]. $\qquad\square$

There are some important shortcomings of the limited fluctuation theory. We restrict ourselves to mention them briefly; for a discussion see [Alb81] and [Nor79]. For instance, the question how the deviation $\varepsilon = p\mu$ and the probability α should be chosen remains open. Further, the similarity of risks (they have the same levels of tariff variables) – though the risks are actually different – is not being taken into account. In this context, [Boo91] points out that not the entire information basis which is available is being taken into account for calculation purposes. Eventually, this leads to a tariff system where the individual pricing is separated from other risks. The following approach which is due to [Bue67] removes these weak points.

2.3.2 Greatest Accuracy Theory – a Bayesian Approach

For a rigorous statement of the model and the derivation of formulae see [DPP94], Section 6.5.4, particularly equation (6.5.24). Within the framework of this Bayesian approach, we observe a single risk over t time periods. Let us first introduce some notation: θ is a "risk parameter" (thought as random variable

with known distribution) describing the risk under consideration. Next, it is assumed that the risk is observed over t time
periods in which it produces claims with identically distributed
claim sizes $X_1, \ldots, X_t$ (with realizations $x_1, \ldots, x_t \in \mathbb{R}$) on
a probability space $(\Omega, \mathcal{A}, P)$ being conditionally independent,
given θ. We write $\bar{X}_t := \frac{X_1 + \cdots + X_t}{t}$. Further, $\hat{\pi}$ denotes the
estimate for

$$\mu(\theta) := E(X_i | \theta),$$

the (unknown) risk premium (it is assumed that the expected
claim sizes are equal for all periods). Finally, let $\mu := E(\mu(\theta)) = E(E(X_i | \theta)) = E(X_i) = E(\bar{X})$ be the expected risk premium
and $\sigma^2(\theta) := V(X_i | \theta)$. The goal is to find the best estimate
$\hat{\pi}$ for the unknown risk premium $\mu(\theta)$. Theoretically, the best
estimate for $\mu(\theta)$ can be shown to be the following conditional
expectation.

Remark 2.3.3 *A credibility premium $\hat{\pi}$ is **exact** if for all other
credibility premiums π the inequality*

$$E\left((\hat{\pi} - \mu(\theta))^2\right) \leq E\left((\pi - \mu(\theta))^2\right)$$

holds.

$$\hat{\pi} := E\left(\mu(\theta) \mid X_1 = x_1, \ldots, X_t = x_t\right)$$

is an exact credibility premium.

Proof. See [vSc89]. $\qquad\qquad\qquad\qquad\qquad\qquad\qquad\square$

Unfortunately, this conditional expectation can be calculated
only with help of additional information on the distribution of
the random vector $(\theta, X_1, \ldots, X_t)$. But if we restrict ourselves
to a linear combination according to

$$\hat{\pi} = a_0 + a_1 X_1 + \cdots + a_t X_t,$$

such a best *linear* approximation of $\mu(\theta)$ can be found in the
sense of a minimum mean squared error

$$MSE := E\left((\hat{\pi} - \mu(\theta))^2\right).$$

This motivates the following

Definition 2.3.4 *Let* $a_0, \ldots, a_t, x_1, \ldots, x_t$ *be real numbers. The map*

$$(x_1, \ldots, x_t) \mapsto a_0 + a_1 x_1 + \cdots + a_t x_t$$

is referred to as **(linear) credibility premium** *if the following condition holds.*
$\forall b_0, \ldots, b_t \in \mathbb{R}:$

$$E\left((a_0 + a_1 X_1 + \cdots + a_t X_t - \mu(\theta))^2\right)$$
$$\leq E\left((b_0 + b_1 X_1 + \cdots + b_t X_t - \mu(\theta))^2\right).$$

As a result of finding such a linear premium, one ends up with the credibility premium given in the following statement.

Proposition 2.3.5 *The premium*

$$\hat{\pi} = \gamma_t \bar{X}_t + (1 - \gamma_t)\mu \tag{2.7}$$

where the corresponding credibility weight is given by

$$\gamma_t = \frac{V(\mu(\theta))}{V(\mu(\theta)) + \frac{E(\sigma^2(\theta))}{t}} \tag{2.8}$$

is a credibility premium.

Proof. See [DPP94]. $\qquad\square$

The framework in which formula (2.8) has been developed is referred to as **Bühlmann model**. The credibility premium has the following desirable properties, cf. [vSc89].

(a) Since $0 \leq \gamma_t \leq 1$, the estimator for the premium lies between the arithmetic mean of the observed claim sizes of the considered risk and the average claim size of the collective. Moreover, when we raise the number of observations t, higher credibility is obtained according to (2.8):

$$\gamma_t \longrightarrow 1 \quad \text{for} \quad t \longrightarrow \infty.$$

This is desirable, since – according to the strong law of large numbers – the average claim size (over the t periods) converges P-a.s. towards the risk adequate premium.

(b) The higher $V(\mu(\theta))$, i.e. the more heterogeneous the collective, the higher the credibility factor γ_t.

(c) Similarly, the higher $E(\sigma^2(\theta))$, i.e. the more claim sizes of a particular risk vary, the lower its credibility.

(d) The credibility premium $\hat{\pi}$ is unbiased (with respect to P); more precisely, we have

$$E(\hat{\pi}) = E\left(\mu(\theta)\right) = E(X_i).$$

(e) As the credibility factor γ_t lies between 0 and 1, the variance does not vary more than than the average claim size, formally:

$$V\left(\hat{\pi} \,|\, \theta = \vartheta\right) \leq V\left(\bar{X}_t \,|\, \theta = \vartheta\right)$$

for all risk parameters ϑ. This results immediately from (2.7). Moreover, it follows that the variance of the credibility premium converges towards zero when the number of periods increases.

The optimality aspect makes credibility estimators interesting for our examination of classification methods later on. As far as we are concerned in our investigation, we can leave the treatment of credibility theory at these few remarks; important for our later ideas is solely the aspect of weighting various pieces of claim information to obtain optimal estimators.

Chapter 3

Cluster Analysis in Actuarial Mathematics

3.1   Motivation

Let n, $k \in \mathbb{N}$ throughout and let $\mathcal{K}$ be a non-empty finite set with $|\mathcal{K}| =: n$. Hence there exists a bijective map $f : \mathcal{K} := \{x_1, \ldots, x_n\} \longrightarrow \mathbb{N}_n$; for instance, f may be defined by $x_i \mapsto f(x_i) = i$. In our context, we shall think of $\mathcal{K}$ as a set of *objects* and of $\mathbb{N}_n$ as an index set, and each object has a certain index. Specifically, we characterize the objects by real m-tuples and thus have $\mathcal{K} \subset \mathbb{R}^m$ in our applications.

Definition 3.1.1 *A decomposition $\mathcal{C} := \{C_1, \ldots, C_k\}$, $C_1, \ldots, C_k \subset \mathbb{N}_n$, is a* **partition (of length k)** *or a k-**partition** of $\mathbb{N}_n$, if the following conditions hold:*

   (i) $C_i \neq \emptyset$ $(i = 1, \ldots, k)$

   (ii) $\mathbb{N}_n = \bigcup_{i=1}^{k} C_i$

   (iii) $C_i \cap C_j = \emptyset$ $((i,j) \in \mathbb{N}_n^2,\, i \neq j)$.

The sets $C_1, \ldots, C_k$ are referred to as **clusters** *or* **classes**. *The elements of $\mathcal{K}$ are referred to as* **objects**, *and $\mathcal{K}$ itself is the* **object set**.

Thus obviously, we have $k \leq n$. Each element of $\mathbb{N}_n$ – hence $\mathcal{K}$ – is assigned exactly[1] one cluster, and there are no empty clusters. For the sake of simplification, we shall refer to the corresponding set of elements of $\mathcal{K}$ as clusters as well, e.g. if a cluster is given by $C = \{2, 5\}$, we identify C with the corresponding set of objects $\{x_2, x_5\}$. Consequently, we refer to partitions of $\mathbb{N}_n$ as partitions of $\mathcal{K}$. Alternatively, clusters can be represented as (ordered) tuples $(x_1, \ldots, x_s)$ of natural numbers (or objects, respectively). In what follows, we prefer their representation as sets.

Definition 3.1.2 *Let $\mathcal{K}$ be a set with n elements: $|\mathcal{K}| = n$. The number of k-partitions of $\mathcal{K}$ is denoted by $S(n, k)$ and referred to as* **Stirling number of the second kind**.

To calculate $S(n, k)$, we need the following lemma, see [Jac83].

Lemma 3.1.3 *For n, $k \in \mathbb{N}$, the Stirling numbers of the second kind obey*

$$S(n + 1, k) = S(n, k - 1) + kS(n, k).$$

Proof. There are $S(n + 1, k)$ partitions of length k of the set $\{x_1, \ldots, x_{n+1}\}$. Exactly two possibilities to group the $(n + 1)$th element x_{n+1} can arise: Either (i) $\{x_{n+1}\}$ defines a whole cluster or (ii) x_{n+1} belongs to some cluster containing other elements as well. The first possibility occurs in $S(n, k - 1)$ ways, whereas the second possibility occurs in $kS(n, k)$ ways. Since there are no other possibilities to group the $n + 1$th element, the claim follows. $\square$

---

[1] We restrict ourselves to *exhaustive* ("crisp") clusterings. In *fuzzy* clustering, an object may belong to more than one cluster with varying membership grade.

n \ k	2	3	4	5	10
2	1	0	0	0	0
3	3	1	0	0	0
4	7	6	1	0	0
5	15	25	10	1	0
10	511	9,330	34,105	179,487	1
15	16,383	2,375,101	42,355,950	$2.734 \cdot 10^9$	12,662,650
20	524,289	580,606,446	$4.523 \cdot 10^{10}$	$4.306 \cdot 10^{12}$	$5.918 \cdot 10^{12}$
25	$1.678 \cdot 10^7$	$1.412 \cdot 10^{11}$	$4.677 \cdot 10^{13}$	$3.703 \cdot 10^{16}$	$1.203 \cdot 10^{18}$
50	$5,631 \cdot 10^{14}$	$1.196 \cdot 10^{23}$	$5.285 \cdot 10^{28}$	$7.401 \cdot 10^{32}$	$2.616 \cdot 10^{43}$
100	$6,342 \cdot 10^{29}$	$8.590 \cdot 10^{46}$	$6.704 \cdot 10^{56}$	$2.316 \cdot 10^{69}$	$2.756 \cdot 10^{93}$

Table 3.1: Stirling numbers of the second kind for selected values of n and k

Additionally, one defines $S(0,0) := 1$, $S(0,1) = S(0,2) = \cdots :=$ 0. Using the recursion formula of the lemma, we obtain the following explicite expression for the Stirling numbers of the second kind.

Proposition 3.1.4 *The Stirling numbers of the second kind are given by*

$$S(n,k) = \frac{1}{k!} \sum_{j=0}^{k} (-1)^{k-j} \binom{k}{j} j^n.$$

Proof. Induction (apply Lemma 3.1.3). □

Table 3.1.4 shows that there are immense numbers of possibilities to divide even very small and manageable sets into disjoint and exhaustive subsets. For comparison observe that the number of nucleons in the universe is of magnitude 10^{82}, see [Fis05], and the big bang occurred no more than 10^{18} seconds ago.

We take a closer look at the following two situations: (i) the number of classes k is not fixed in advance and (ii) not only the number k of classes, but also the cardinalities κ_i $(i = 1, \ldots, k)$ of each cluster are fixed in advance.

n	$B(n)$	n	$B(n)$
1	1	9	21,147
2	2	10	115,975
3	5	15	$1.382 \cdot 10^9$
4	15	20	$5.172 \cdot 10^{13}$
5	52	25	$4.638 \cdot 10^{18}$
6	203	30	$8.467 \cdot 10^{23}$
7	877	40	$1.574 \cdot 10^{35}$
8	4,140	50	$1.857 \cdot 10^{47}$

Table 3.2: Bell numbers for some values of n

Situation (i): If the number k of subsets is not specified in advance, there are of course

$$B(n) := \sum_{i=1}^{n} S(n, i) \tag{3.1}$$

partitions of a set with cardinality n.

Definition 3.1.5 *The number $B(n)$ is referred to as nth **Bell number** or **exponential number**.*

Thus $B(n)$ represents the number of *all* partitions of a set having n elements. According to equation (3.1), the numbers given in table 3.1 are the row sums as stated in table 3.1.4.

Situation (ii): [BG04] and [BG07] recently proposed a clustering algorithm which requires the input of the number of clusters and their cardinalities. Again, we wish to judge the magnitude of the number of all clustering results in this special case, cf. [Boc74]. W.l.o.g., we can assume the cluster cardinalities κ_i $(i = 1, \ldots, k)$ to be listed in descending order:

$$\kappa_1 \geq \kappa_2 \geq \cdots \geq \kappa_k (\geq 1).$$

Definition 3.1.6 *In this case of ordered cardinalities we refer to the k-tuple*

$$(\kappa_1, \ldots, \kappa_k)$$

as the **type** of the partition $\{C_1, \ldots, C_k\}$.

Assuming that among these k cardinalities 1 appears exactly m_1 times, 2 appears exactly m_2 times (in general: i appears exactly m_i times for $i = 1, \ldots, k$), i.e. $\sum_{i=1}^{n} i \cdot m_i = n$, where n denotes the cardinality of the set to be clustered, we have the following statement.

Proposition 3.1.7 *A set $\mathcal{K}$ of cardinality n possesses exactly*

$$\frac{n!}{\prod_{i=1}^{k}(\kappa_i!) \prod_{i=1}^{k}(m_i!)}$$

partitions of type $(\kappa_1, \ldots, \kappa_k)$, where m_i indicates how often number i appears among the cardinalities $\kappa_1, \ldots, \kappa_k$.

Proof. The symmetric group S_n of $\mathbb{N}_n$ has $n!$ elements – the number of ways to sort the n elements. Neither we distinguish the $\prod_{i=1}^{k} \kappa_i!$ partitions in which merely the elements (of $\mathcal{K}$) appear in a different sequence within the classes, nor the $\prod_{i=1}^{k} m_i!$ partitions with merely another sequence of classes with same cardinality. Hence the claim follows. $\qquad\square$

Examples 3.1.8 Suppose we are given the set $\mathcal{K} := \mathbb{N}_4$, i.e. $|\mathcal{K}| = n = 4$.

(a) If do not specify the number of classes k, we can partition $\mathcal{K}$ in $B(4) = 15$ different ways.

(b) Choosing $k = 3$ classes, there are $S(4,3) = 6$ possibilities to partition $\mathcal{K}$.

(c) Again choosing $k = 3$ classes, $\mathcal{K}$ has $\frac{4!}{2!1!1!2!1!} = 6$ partitions of type $(\kappa_1, \kappa_2, \kappa_3) = (2, 1, 1)$, namely

$\{\{1,2\},\{3\},\{4\}\}, \quad \{\{1,3\},\{2\},\{4\}\}, \quad \{\{1,4\},\{2\},\{3\}\},$
$\{\{2,3\},\{1\},\{4\}\}, \quad \{\{2,4\},\{1\},\{3\}\}, \quad \{\{3,4\},\{1\},\{2\}\}$

(we have $m_1 = 2$, $m_2 = 1$).

In statistics, *cluster analysis* solves the problem of partitioning a given data set into *homogeneous* (with respect to some pre-defined characteristics) subsets, the clusters. The

$$n \text{ objects}$$

alongside their observed

$$m \text{ characteristics}$$

are usually collected in a data matrix

$$X := (x_{ij})_{\substack{i=1,\ldots,n \\ j=1,\ldots,m}} \in \mathbb{R}^{n \times m}$$

where the ith row x_{ij} $(1 \le j \le m)$ represents object i $(1 \le i \le n)$ – each object is considered an element of $\mathbb{R}^m$. The result of a cluster analysis is expressed by an n-tuple $(\iota_1, \ldots, \iota_n) \in \{1, \ldots, k\}^n$ where $\iota_i = j$ means that the ith object belongs to the jth cluster.

As mentioned above, the purpose of cluster analysis is to find the "most homogeneous" partition of a data set. Against this background, two questions arise immediately: (i) How to measure similarity/distance of objects and thus to judge the homogeneity of the clusters and (ii) how to obtain an "optimal" partition? We take a closer look at these aspects in the following three sections.

As for answering question (ii), one could could demand looking at *all* partitions of a given data set $\mathcal{K}$ and judge each partition by some measure of homogeneity and select the best one. However, as the stated numbers of $S(n, k)$ and $B(n)$ indicate, such a *total enumeration*, i.e. the analysis of the entire set of partitions, is not feasable, particularly as real world data sets are concerned.

3.2 Distance and Similarity

A variety of concepts covering the measurement of distances among all types of variables (nominal, ordinal, metric) is contained in almost every textbook on cluster analysis. We restrict ourselves to the case of metric variables and thus review some facts about the metric strucure of $\mathbb{R}^m$. Endowed with a norm, this set forms the space cluster analysis works in.

3.2.1 Object Distance

Definition 3.2.1 *Let V be a vector space over $\mathbb{R}$. A* **norm** *is a map*

$$\| \, \| : V \longrightarrow \mathbb{R}, \quad x \mapsto \|x\|$$

such that the following conditions hold:
$\forall x, y \in V \quad \forall \lambda \in \mathbb{R}:$

   (i) $\|x\| = 0 \Longleftrightarrow x = 0$ *(definiteness)*

   (ii) $\|\lambda x\| = |\lambda| \, \|x\|$ *(positive homogeneity)*

   (iii) $\|x + y\| \leq \|x\| + \|y\|$ *(triangle inequality).*

Hence, $\|x\| \geq 0$ for all $x \in V$. In our applications, we have $V := \mathbb{R}^m$ throughout. The following example presents an important class of norms on $\mathbb{R}^m$.

Example 3.2.2 Let $1 \leq p < \infty$. For $x =^t (x_1, \ldots, x_m) \in \mathbb{R}^m$, the *p-norm* is defined by

$$\|x\|_p := \left(\sum_{\mu=1}^{m} |x_\mu|^p \right)^{\frac{1}{p}}.$$

Obviously, $\| \, \|_p$ obeys conditions (i) and (ii) of definition 3.2.1. The Minkowski inequality yields that condition (iii) is satisfied as well. A special case is the frequently used Euclidean norm $\|x\|_2 = \sqrt{\langle x, x \rangle}$; here, $\langle x, y \rangle =^t x \cdot y$ denotes the *canonical scalar product.*

The p-norm can be extended in a natural way.

Example 3.2.3 The *maximum norm* $\|\ \|_\infty$ is given by

$$\|x\|_\infty := \max\{|x_1|, \ldots, |x_m|\}$$

for $x =^t (x_1, \ldots, x_m) \in \mathbb{R}^m$.

We may interprete the maximum norm as limit of the p-norm.

Remark 3.2.4 *Letting* $\|x\|_\infty = \max\{|x_1|, \ldots, |x_m|\}$, *we have*

$$\|x\|_\infty = \lim_{p \to \infty} \|x\|_p.$$

Proof.

(i) Obviously, the maximum of $\{|x_1|, \ldots, |x_m|\}$ exists. Further, we have

$$\|x\|_\infty \le |x_1| + \cdots + |x_m|$$

and since $p \ge 1$, this yields

$$\|x\|_\infty^p \le |x_1|^p + \cdots + |x_m|^p.$$

On taking the p-th root, we obtain

$$\|x\|_\infty \le \|x\|_p.$$

(ii) Next, the inequality

$$|x_1|^p + \cdots + |x_m|^p \le m\|x\|_\infty^p$$

holds, from which

$$\|x\|_p \le m^{\frac{1}{p}}\|x\|_\infty$$

follows.

Thus we have proved the inequalities

$$\|x\|_\infty \le \|x\|_p \le m^{\frac{1}{p}} \|x\|_\infty.$$

On taking the limit for $p \longrightarrow \infty$, we obtain

$$\|x\|_\infty \le \lim_{p\to\infty} \|x\|_p \le \|x\|_\infty,$$

yielding equality and completing the proof. □

We use norms to define a distance measure between two elements of an arbitrary set. We need to following – very general – term.

Definition 3.2.5 *Let M be a nonempty set. A **metric** on M is a map*

$$d : M \times M \longrightarrow \mathbb{R}, \quad (x,y) \mapsto d(x,y)$$

when the following conditions hold:
$\forall x, y, z \in M$

(i) $d(x,y) = 0 \iff x = y$ *(definiteness)*

(ii) $d(x,y) = d(y,x)$ *(symmetry)*

(iii) $d(x,z) \le d(x,y) + d(y,z)$ *(triangle inequality).*

Observe that $d(x,y) \ge 0$ for all $x,y \in M$.

The next example demonstrates how norms can be used to define a metric.

Example 3.2.6 Let $(V, \|\ \|)$ be a normed real vector space. Then
$$d(x,y) := \|x - y\|$$
for $x, y \in V$ defines a metric on V. This follows immediately from the respective properties of a norm.

66

Definition 3.2.7 *We say that $\| \ \|$ in example 3.2.6* **induces** *the metric d. The metric space (V, d) is referred to as* **Minkowski space**.

Thus $\|x\| = d(x, 0_V)$ for all $x \in V$, i.e. the distance between x and the zero element 0_V of V is given by $\|x\|$.

As far as cluster analysis is concerned, a particularly important class of distance measures are the *Minkowski metrics* defined by $d_p(x, y) := \|x - y\|_p$ where $1 \le p \le \infty$. These maps are induced by the respective p-norms. Special cases (or extentions, respectively) are the

- d_1, the Manhattan metric
- d_2, the Euclidian distance
- d_∞, the Chebychev metric.

The most familiar metric is d_2 as it descibes distances according to intuition. We mention two properties of the Euclidian distance d_2, see [Boc74] or [SL77].

(a) d_2 is invariant under congruences, i.e. under maps $\tau \circ f$, where τ is a translation and f is an orthogonal map:
$$d_2(\tau + f(x), \tau + f(y)) = \|f(x) - f(y)\|_2 = \|f(x - y)\|_2$$
$$= \|x - y\|_2 = d_2(x, y).$$

(b) d_2 is not scale invariant, it is thus important to have "comparable" units to measure the m variables. If this is not the case, the variables have to be standardized; see [Boc74] for standardization methods.

As for the p-norms, it can be shown that they are neither invariant under orthogonal maps nor that they are scale invariant, see [Boc74]. They are solely invariant under translations.

The p-norms are a generalization of the Euclidian norm $\| \ \|_2$. Another generalization of the Euclidian norm is obtained by the following definition, see [SL77] or [Spä77].

Definition 3.2.8 *Let*

$$\|x\|_B := \sqrt{{}^t x B x}$$

for $x \in \mathbb{R}^m$ and positive definite $B \in \mathbb{R}^{m \times m}$. Then the expression

$$d_B(x, y) = \sqrt{{}^t(x - y) B (x - y)}$$

is referred to as **quadratic distance function**.

Remark 3.2.9 $\| \ \|_B$ *is a norm and thus induces the metric d_B.*

Proof. We have to verify the conditions from definition 3.2.1.
(i), (ii): trivial.
(iii): We have

$$\|x + y\|_B = \sqrt{{}^t x B x + {}^t y B y} = \sqrt{\|x\|_B^2 + \|y\|_B^2} \leq \|x\|_B + \|y\|_B$$

where the last inequality follows from $\sqrt{a + b} \leq \sqrt{a} + \sqrt{b}$ for $a, b \geq 0$. This completes the proof. $\square$

For instance, choosing $B := I_m$, where I_m is the unit matrix, leads to the metric d_2.

Not any metric on $\mathbb{R}^m$ is a suitable distance measure in terms of its applicability to statistical methods. For instance, look at the *discrete metric*, defined by

$$d_{dis}(x, y) := \begin{cases} 0 & (x = y) \\ 1 & (x \neq y). \end{cases}$$

Points have distance 1 as long as they are not equal. Clearly, this measure is too "rough" for clustering purposes.

We now show how a matrix B can be chosen such that the metric from definition 3.2.8 leads to a notably meaningful distance measure: The following special choice of B yields a metric with a favourable property. Therefore, we need the (empirical) covariance matrix of our m characteristics entering the cluster analysis, given by

$$S := (s_{kj})_{1 \leq k,j \leq m} := \left(\frac{1}{n} \sum_{i=1}^{n} (x_{ik} - \bar{x}_{\cdot k})(x_{ij} - \bar{x}_{\cdot j}) \right)_{1 \leq k,j \leq m}$$
$$\in \mathbb{R}^{m \times m},$$

where s_{kj} denotes the empirical covariance between variables k and j, i.e. $x_{\cdot k}$ denotes the kth column of the data matrix X and $\bar{x}_{\cdot k} := \sum_{i=1}^{n} x_{ik}$ is the arithmetic mean of the kth characteristic and n is the number of objects. In case S is invertible, we may consider the following distance measure. Observe that S then is positive definite as well since it can easily be rewritten as a product

$$S = \frac{1}{n} {}^{t}AA$$

(see [Spä77]) for invertible A, i.e.

$${}^{t}xSx = {}^{t}x(\frac{1}{\sqrt{n}} A \frac{1}{\sqrt{n}} A)x = \frac{1}{n} {}^{t}(Ax)Ax > 0$$

for $x \neq 0$. It follows that S^{-1} is positive definite as well. We have proved

Proposition 3.2.10 *The map* $d_{Mah} : \mathbb{R}^m \times \mathbb{R}^m \longrightarrow \mathbb{R}$ *defined by*

$$d_{Mah}(x,y) := d_{S^{-1}}(x,y) = \|x - y\|_{S^{-1}} = \sqrt{{}^{t}(x-y)S^{-1}(x-y)}$$

is a metric. It is referred to as **Mahalanobis distance**. $\square$

In the light of statistical analyses, this distance measure has the following desirable property: While the Euclidian distance is in general invariant only under congruences, the main property of d_{Mah} is its invariance under arbitrary nonsingular maps

$$x_i \mapsto Cx_i + a =: y_i \quad (1 \leq i \leq n)$$

(i.e. object x_i is mapped onto $Cx_i + a$) where $C \in \mathbb{R}^{m \times m}$ and $\det C \neq 0$ and fixed $a \in \mathbb{R}^m$, and where C needs not be orthogonal, see [Boc74]. We prove the latter statement. The m characteristics of the n mapped objects $y_1, \ldots, y_n$ have covariance matrix $\tilde{S} := CS^tC$, hence $\tilde{S}^{-1} =^t C^{-1}S^{-1}C^{-1}$. Thus we have

$$
\begin{aligned}
d_{Mah}(y_i, y_j) &= d_{\tilde{S}^{-1}}(y_i, y_j) \\
&= \sqrt{^t(y_i - y_j)\tilde{S}^{-1}(y_i - y_j)} \\
&= \sqrt{^t(x_i - x_j)^tC^tC^{-1}S^{-1}C^{-1}C(x_i - x_j)} \\
&= \sqrt{^t(x_i - x_j)S^{-1}(x_i - x_j)} = d_{Mah}(x_i, x_j)
\end{aligned}
$$

In terms of statistics, this property implies *scale invariance* of d_{Mah}: Suppose therefore that $C := diag(c_1, \ldots, c_m) \in \mathbb{R}^{m \times m}$ is a diagonal matrix with nonzero diagonal elements and assume further that $a = 0$. In this case, the transformation

$$
x_i \mapsto Cx_i =: y_i \quad (1 \leq i \leq n)
$$

is the multiplication of variable j with constant c_j $(1 \leq j \leq m)$ and is commonly known as *scaling*. The above stated invariance property thus expresses that it is unimportant how the characteristics (i.e. in which units) are quoted.

3.2.2 Cluster Distance

So far, we have discussed measuring the distance between single objects, which are elements of the clusters. We now turn to the measurement of the distance of the clusters themselves. We consider clusters $C, D \subset \mathbb{R}^m$ and denote our cluster distance measures by *dist*. We have seen that distances between objects are nonnegative real numbers. Likewise, the distance between two clusters ought to be a nonnegative real number.

As clusters may contain of only one object, the case of measuring distances between objects and clusters is included in a natural way. Let us say the distance between an object x and a cluster C is the distance between a cluster containing object x and C. In what follows, we shall motivate and present some common distance measures.

Cluster distances based on object distances

Let us tie in with what we have just pointed out, namely with measuring the distance $dist(x, C)$ between a point $x \in \mathbb{R}^m$ and a subset $C \subset \mathbb{R}^m$. One possibility would be to define

$$dist(x, C) := \inf\{d(x, c) \mid c \in C\},$$

where d is a metric on $\mathbb{R}^m$, see [For06]. This measure has the following desirable property.

Proposition 3.2.11 *Let d be a metric on $\mathbb{R}^m$. The function $x \mapsto dist(x, C)$ is continuous on $\mathbb{R}^m$.*

Proof. We have $dist(x', C) \leq d(x', x) + dist(x, C)$ and hence

$$|dist(x, C) - dist(x', C)| < \varepsilon \quad \text{for} \quad d(x, x') < \varepsilon.$$

Thus the continuity follows by the ε–δ–criterion. $\qquad\square$

Based on this consideration, one can define the distance between two clusters D, C in the following way, cf. [For06]:

$$
\begin{aligned}
dist(D, C) &:= \inf\{dist(x, C) \mid x \in D\} \\
&= \inf\{d(x, y) \mid x \in D,\, y \in C\}.
\end{aligned}
$$

Here, the underlying idea is to measure distances of sets by object distances, i.e. by distances of their elements. Using this definition of the distance between two clusters, we can show the following property.

Proposition 3.2.12 *If $C \cap D = \emptyset$ and if C and D are bounded[2] in $\mathbb{R}^m$, we have*

$$dist(D, C) > 0.$$

Proof. By the Heine-Borel theorem, C and D are compact (note that C and D are finite since the set which is to be clustered is finite, see definition 3.1.1), particularly, they are closed. According to the Weierstrass theorem regarding the existence of extrema, there is a point $p \in D$ for which the continuous map $x \mapsto dist(x, C)$ takes its minimum, i.e.

$$dist(p, C) = dist(D, C).$$

Since C is closed, $\mathbb{R}^m \setminus C$ is open, hence there exists $\varepsilon > 0$ and neighbourhood $B_\varepsilon(p) \subset \mathbb{R}^m \setminus C$. Hence $dist(p, C) = dist(D, C) \geq \varepsilon > 0$. $\square$

In terms of our normed space $(\mathbb{R}^m, \| \, \|)$, we may define the following distance measure for clusters

$$C := \{x_1, \ldots, x_s\} \quad \text{and} \quad D := \{y_1, \ldots, y_t\}.$$

Definition 3.2.13 *The expression*

$$dist_{sing}(C, D) := \inf_{i \leq s, \, j \leq t} \|x_i - y_j\|$$

is referred to as **single-linkage- *or* nearest-neighbour-distance between C and D.**

Thus $dist_{sing}(C, D)$ is the **minimum** distance between objects belonging to C and D.

We now present some other commonly used cluster distance measures based on distances between objects, cf. [Ber81]. The

---

[2] A subset $C \subset \mathbb{R}^m$ is *bounded* if it is contained in a sufficiently big ball, i.e. if there exists $r > 0$ with $\|x\| \leq r$ for all $x \in C$. In applications, we deal with bounded data sets only.

complete-linkage- or *furthest-neighbour*-distance is the **maximum** distance of objects:

$$d_{comp}(C, D) := \sup_{i \leq s, \, j \leq t} \|x_i - y_j\|.$$

Usually, the single-linkage-distance is often considered too small while the complete-linkage-distance is considered too high. The *group-average*-distance **averages** all $s \cdot t$ object distances:

$$d_{group}(C, D) := \frac{1}{st} \sum_{i \leq s, \, j \leq t} \|x_i - y_j\|.$$

Therefore, $d_{group}(C, D)$ lies between $d_{sing}(C, D)$ and $d_{comp}(C, D)$.

Representative distances

Above, we used some particular elements of clusters to derive cluster distances. Now we shall present another important concept.

A cluster $C = \{x_1, \ldots, x_s\}$ can be characterized in an obvious way by its *centre of gravity*

$$c := \frac{1}{s} \sum_{i=1}^{s} x_i \in \mathbb{R}^m,$$

also known as its *centroid*. Let us now identify clusters with their centroids.

Definition 3.2.14 *Let the centroids of C and D be denoted by c and d, respectively. The expression*

$$dist_{cen}(C, D) := \|c - d\|$$

is referred to as **centroid**-*distance.*

Identifying clusters with their centroids, $dist_{cen}$ yields a *continuous* distance measure since the map $diff$, defined by $diff(c, d) :=$

73

$c - d$ is continuous and the norm is (actually Lipschitz) continuous and $dist_{cen}$ is the composition $\| \ \| \circ diff$.

A *Mahalanobis*-distance can be derived for clusters as well:

$$dist_{Mah}(C, D) = \sqrt{^t(c - d)S^{-1}(c - d)}$$

if S is an invertible covariance matrix obtained from the involved clusters. There are various ways to define S, normally one takes

$$S := \frac{1}{s + t - 2} \left(\sum_i (x_i - c)^t (x_i - c) + \sum_j (y_j - d)^t (y_j - d) \right)$$

$$\in \mathbb{R}^{m \times m}.$$

Properties of Cluster Distances

By means of metrics and norms, the measurement of distances between points does not pose serious problems. However, if we are to define a cluster distance $dist$, the question arises which characteristics we demand. [Hob03] discusses desirable properties of cluster distances. We list some of the most ostensive attributes. Therefore, let $C, D, E \subset \mathbb{R}^m$ be clusters and suppose $C := \{x_1, \ldots, x_s\}$.

(a) fundamental properties

- *symmetry*: $dist(C, D) = dist(D, C)$
- *definiteness*: $dist(C, D) = 0 \iff C = D$
- *properness*: $dist(C, D) = 0 \implies dist(C, E) = dist(D, E)$

(b) geometric properties

- *invariance toward scalar multiplication*: $dist(aC, aD) = dist(C, D)$ $(a > 0)$, where aC denotes $\{ax_1, \ldots, ax_s\}$
- alternatively, one can demand *linear equivariance*: $dist(aC, aD) = a \, dist(C, D)$

- *invariance toward translation*:
  $dist(v + C, v + D) = dist(C, D)$ $(v \in \mathbb{R}^m)$, where $v + C$ denotes $\{v + x_1, \ldots, v + x_s\}$

(c) *triangle inequality*: $dist(C, E) \leq dist(C, D) + dist(D, E)$

(d) behaviour under fusion

- *fusion subadditivity*: $dist(C, D \cup E) \leq dist(C, D) + dist(C, E)$
- *space conserving*: $\min\{dist(C, D), dist(C, E)\} \leq dist(C, D \cup E) \leq \max\{dist(C, D), dist(C, E)\}$
- *weak fusion contraction*:
  $dist(C, D \cup E) \leq \max\{dist(C, D), dist(C, E)\}$
- *fusion contraction*:
  $dist(C, D \cup E) \leq \min\{dist(C, D), dist(C, E)\}$
- *weak space dilatation*:
  $dist(C, D \cup E) \geq \min\{dist(C, D), dist(C, E)\}$
- *space dilatation*: $dist(C, D \cup E)$
  $\geq \max\{dist(C, D), dist(C, E)\}$

(e) other properties

- *invariance toward extension of the arithmetic mean*:
  $dist(C \cup \{c\}, D) = dist(C, D)$, where c is the centroid of C
- *norm compatibility*: *dist* is norm compatible, if the distance between one-elementic clusters defines a norm. If so, one sets

$$\|x - y\| := dist(\{x\}, \{y\})$$

for $x, y \in \mathbb{R}^m$.

We think the listed attributes deserve no further explanation here and pass on a detailed discussion. [Hob03] gives an overview with respect to mutual dependencies among these characteristics and analyzes which commonly used distance functions obey which properties.

3.2.3 Cluster Inhomogeneity

By clustering a set of data it is hoped to obtain homogeneous subsets. In other words, the distances between objects belonging to the same cluster ought to be small. To compare various clusters regarding their heterogeneity, one assigns cluster C a nonnegative real number $\eta(C)$, where η increases when the heterogeneity of C increases. In the following definition, we look at objects from $\mathbb{R}^m$; the set $\cup_{\nu=1}^{\infty}(\mathbb{R}^m)^\nu$ is the space of data sets.

Definition 3.2.15 *A* **cluster inhomogeneity** *is a map* $\eta : \cup_{\nu=1}^{\infty}(\mathbb{R}^m)^\nu \longrightarrow [0, \infty[$.

Like cluster distance measures, heterogeneity measures can be based upon object distances. We list the most important cluster inhomogeneities, cf. [Hob03].

Cluster inhomogeneities based on object distances

(a) Again, let c denote the centroid of cluster C. The *empirical variance* is defined by $\eta(C) := s_C^2 := \frac{1}{n}\sum_{i \leq n}\|x_i - c\|_2^2$. Often, the standard deviation $s_C := \sqrt{s_C^2}$ is used as well.

(b) *group average inhomogeneity*: $\eta(C) := \frac{1}{n(n-1)}\sum_{i,j \leq n}\|x_i - x_j\|$. Observe there are $\binom{n}{2}$ object pairs in C. This figure computes thus the average pairwise distance between the points.

(c) *diameter*: $\eta(C) := diam(C) := \sup_{i,j \leq n}\|x_i - x_j\|$

Volume-based cluster inhomogeneities

Besides basing these considerations upon object distances, there are other possibilities as well, e.g. volume-based measures like the following proposal. Note therefore that the convex hull of a cluster is measurable since it is closed.

$$\eta(C) := \lambda^m(conv(C)) = \int_{conv(C)} d\lambda^m,$$

the m-dimensional Borel-Lebesgue-measure of the convex hull $conv(C)$ of C. This integral exists since $conv(C)$ is compact and the characteristic function $1_{conv(C)}$ is continuous on $conv(C)$. However, if all points lie in a hyperplane $H \subset \mathbb{R}^m$ (i.e. H and hence $conv(C)$ are λ^m- null sets) this results in zero inhomogeneity though the points may be different from each other.

We now develop another idea of a volume-based cluster inhomogeneity and show that this suggestion traces back to an already presented distance-based measure, namely the diameter. Let η be given by the *volume of the smallest ball B containing all points of a cluster*. This is a well traceable, intuitive measure. Due to the triangle inequality, the centre of such a ball is the centre point of the segment connecting the two most remote points of the cluster. Hence the volume of B is given by

$$\lambda^m(B) = \sup_{i,j \le n} \|x_i - x_j\|^m \tau_m$$

where $\tau_m = \frac{\pi^{m/2}}{\Gamma(\frac{m}{2}+1)}$ is the volume of the m-dimensional unit ball. This expression depends decisively on $\sup_{i,j \le n} \|x_i - x_j\|$, and the latter figure is the commonly used diameter, hence this yields an equivalent measure.

Properties of Cluster Inhomogeneities

We now come to the question of plausible properties of cluster inhomogeneity measures. Some desirable properties of cluster inhomogenities are

(a) fundamental properties

- *unboundedness*: there is no constant $const$ with $\eta(C) \le const$ for all clusters C

- *definiteness*: $\eta(C) = 0 \Longleftrightarrow C = \{x\}$, i.e. all objects are identical with respect to their characteristics.[3]

(b) geometric properties

- *translation invariance*: $\eta(v + C) = \eta(C)$ $(v \in \mathbb{R}^m)$
- *linear equivariance toward scalar multiplication*: $\eta(aC) = a\eta(C)$ $(a \in \mathbb{R})$

(c) behaviour under fusion

- *fusion supra additivity*: $\eta(C \cup D) \geq \eta(C) + \eta(D)$
- *weak fusion supra monotony*: $\eta(C \cup D)$ $\geq \min\{\eta(C), \eta(D)\}$
- *strong fusion supra monotony*: $\eta(C \cup D)$ $\geq \max\{\eta(C), \eta(D)\}$

(d) *contraction by extension of the arithmetic mean* c: $\eta(C \cup \{c\}) \leq \eta(C)$.

When we describe a cluster as a tuple $(x_1, \ldots, x_s)$, we can require that its inhomogeneity does not change when an object x_i is duplicated, i.e.

$$\eta((x_1, \ldots, x_s, x_i)) = \eta((x_1, \ldots, x_s)).$$

We shall not explain these statements in detail as they have a clear meaning. For a comprehensive discussion of these attributes see [Hob03].

3.3   Cluster Criterions

Now we come to the generation of clusters and shall need the following definition, cf. [Hob03] or [SL77]. Therefore, let $\mathcal{C}_k^n$ denote the set of all k-partitions of $\mathbb{N}_n$.

---

[3]Representing clusters as *tuples* rather than sets would be more suitable to formulate this condition: This leads to $C = (x, \ldots, x)$.

Definition 3.3.1 *A cluster criterion is a real function*

$$z : \{x_1, \ldots, x_n\} \times C_k^n \longrightarrow \mathbb{R}$$

depending upon the data set $\{x_1, \ldots, x_n\} \subset \mathbb{R}^m$ *and the partition* $\mathcal{C} = \{C_1, \ldots, C_k\} \in C_k^n$ *of* $\mathbb{N}_n$,

$$(\{x_1, \ldots, x_n\}, \mathcal{C}) \mapsto z(\{x_1, \ldots, x_n\}, \mathcal{C}).$$

To simplify notation, we shall write $z(\mathcal{C})$ instead of $z(\{x_1, \ldots, x_n\}, \mathcal{C})$ since the data are fixed anyway. Cluster criterions serve to judge various clusterings. In what follows, we use them as **target functions**. For instance, a particular cluster criterion may be constructed in a way that it takes low values for "good" partitions and high values for "bad" ones. In the sense of a cluster analysis, bad partitions consist of heterogeneous sets and good partitions correspond to homogeneous sets. Therefore, we can formulate the task of generating clusters as an **optimization problem**:

$$z(\mathcal{C}) \longrightarrow \min_{\mathcal{C} \in C_k^n},$$

here low values for z are assumed to indicate a good clustering and high values indicate a poor clustering result.

As we have seen, total enumeration, i.e. investigating z for all possible groupings $\mathcal{C}$, fails due to the tremendous number of possibilities, more precisely we have already shown in proposition 3.1.4 that $|\mathcal{C}_k^n| = S(n,k)$. Let us take a look at some commonly used target functions.

Basically, cluster criterions stem from the idea of

(i) minimizing the inhomogeneity of a partition, which we simply define to equal the sum of all cluster inhomogeneities

$$\sum_{j=1}^{k} \eta(C_j) \longrightarrow \min$$

and of

(ii) maximizing the (pairwise) distances between the clusters

$$\sum_{i,j=1}^{k} dist(C_i, C_j) \longrightarrow \max,$$

see [Hob03]. Ideally, a cluster criterion expresses the following items, see [Boc74].

(a) *Homogeneity of C*: How similar are the objects within a certain class?

(b) *Separation of C*: How dissimilar are the objects of different classes and how well are they separated?

(c) Do similar objects belong to the same class, and do dissimilar objects belong to different classes indeed?

The following examples concretize these ideas.

Examples 3.3.2 (a) The *variance* or *k-means criterion*

$$z_1(\mathcal{C}) = \sum_{j=1}^{k} \sum_{i \in C_j} \|x_i - c_j\|_2^2 \longrightarrow \min,$$

$c_j := \frac{1}{|C_j|} \sum_{i \in C_j} x_i$ is the centroid of cluster C_j.[4] This target function is appropriate when the clusters have approximately same cardinality and when they are balls in $\mathbb{R}^m$ of about equal size. Additionally, the variables should be uncorrelated, see [SL77]. Thus long drawn-out clusters will not be identified using this target function. Equivalently, instead of minimizing z_1, one can maximize z_3 defined by:

$$z_3(\mathcal{C}) = \sum_{j=1}^{k} |C_j| \, \|c_j - \bar{c}\|_2^2 \longrightarrow \max,$$

---

[4]The target function $z_2(\mathcal{C}) = \sum_{j=1}^{k} \frac{1}{|C_j|} \sum_{i \in C_j} \|x_i - c_j\|_2^2 \longrightarrow \min$ is plausible as well.

where $\bar{c} := \frac{1}{n} \sum_{i=1}^{n} x_i$ is the average of the entire data, see [Spä77].

(b) Similarly, instead of using the Euclidian distance, a p-norm can be used:

$$z_4(\mathcal{C}) = \sum_{j=1}^{k} \sum_{i \in C_j} \|x_i - c_j\|_p^p \longrightarrow \min,$$

where c_j is an appropriate cluster centre for the target function. In the case $p = 2$, it makes sense to choose the gravity centres (see (a)), whereas for $p = 1$, the vector of the medians is an adequate cluster centre. The case $p = 1$ is particularly important for the location planning of e.g. phone boxes, schools etc. in perpendicular road networks, see [SL77].

(c) Using the Mahalanobis distance suggests the criterion

$$z_5(\mathcal{C}) = \sum_{j=1}^{k} \sum_{i \in C_j} {}^t(x_i - c_j)S^{-1}(x_i - c_j) \longrightarrow \min$$

where c_j is the centre of gravity of the jth cluster.

(d) the *centroid criterion*

$$z_6(\mathcal{C}) = \sum_{j,l} \|c_j - c_l\| \longrightarrow \max$$

(e) the *maximum diameter*

$$z_7(\mathcal{C}) = \max_{j} \sup_{i,l \in C_j} \|x_i - x_l\| \longrightarrow \min$$

(f) the *minimal distance* criterion

$$z_8(\mathcal{C}) = \min_{j,l} \min_{i \in C_j, h \in C_l} \|x_i - x_h\| \longrightarrow \max$$

The previous examples represent merely a sample of criterions. A variety of other target functions can be found in [Boc74], [SL77] and [Spä83].

Finally, we mention that another class of target functions, namely *stochastic* criterions, is used frequently as well, but not discussed here. [Hob03] gives a general survey on such probabilistic models, and [Mac02] presents applications to actuarial problems.

3.4 Clustering Algorithms

We now address algorithms determining an optimum of a cluster criterion z. Generally, an *optimization problem* is the problem to find a minimum(s) or a maximum(s) of a given function $z : D \longrightarrow \mathbb{R}$, possibly with respect to some constraints $g_1(x) \geq 0, \ldots, g_r(x) \geq 0$, where the g_j's are real functions with domain D. Usually, one classifies optimization problems according to the domain D of the target function z and the constraints $g_1, \ldots, g_r$. Since in our applications the domain $D = \mathcal{C}_k^n$ – the set of all k-partitions of $\mathbb{N}_n$ – is finite, we are dealing with **combinatorial optimization problems**.

3.4.1 Heuristic Algorithms

We have stated the cluster analysis problem as an optimization problem and shall now present two general approaches of obtaining acceptable clustering results, i.e. (relatively) optimal values of the target function z. We present some methods as outlined in [SL77]. A comprehensive reference for heuristic algorithms gives [Spä83].

Minimal Distance Methods

1. Select an initial partition.

2. Compute the cluster centres and choose a distance measure *dist*.

3. Shift each element to the group having the nearest – in the sense of *dist* – cluster centre.

4. Continue with 2. or stop, if no element has changed its cluster.

Exchange Methods

1. Select an initial partition.

2. Compute the cluster centres.

3. For each element check whether or not the value of the target function can be improved by shifting it to a different cluster. If so, move the element in question to that cluster with the highest improvement of z. Compute the new cluster centres.

4. Continue with 3. or stop, if there have not occurred any group changes n consecutive times.

One of the most widely used (minimal distance) methods is the *k-means* algorithm, see [And73] or [SL77]. The corresponding target function is z_1, which is to be minimized. The procedure is as follows:

k-means Algorithm

1. Select an initial partition.

2. For each cluster compute its centre of gravity.

3. Assign each object the cluster possessing the nearest – in the sense of the Euclidian distance – cluster centroid. Recompute the centres of gravity after each change of objects for the involved clusters.

4. Continue with 3. or stop, if there has not been a change after n consecutive steps.

This algorithm turns out to converge fast, after only a few iteration steps, a local minimum of z_1 can be obtained. Significant shortcomings of the k-means algorithms – besides that normally no *global* minimum of the cluster criterion is obtained – are that the final partition depends upon

- the initial partition

- the sequence of objects within the data set,

see [SL77] and [And73].

All methods we have described here require the investigator to select a (random) initial partition. To find it, [SL77] suggest taking the following simple technique: Object i is assigned cluster

$$mod(i - 1, k) + 1.$$

By doing so, objects 1, $k + 1$, $2k + 1$ etc. are assigned group 1 initally, objects 2, $k + 2$, $2k + 2$ are assigned group 2 initially, and so forth.

3.4.2 A Quadratic Optimization Model

We outline a recent approach of optimally solving clustering problems, namely the algorithm described in [BG04] or [BG07]. Suppose we are given an object set $\mathcal{K}$ with $n \in \mathbb{N}$ objects. The corresponding index set is thus $\mathbb{N}_n$. As usual, the objects characterized by $m \in \mathbb{N}$ considered variables are represented as vectors $x_1, \ldots, x_n \in \mathbb{R}^m$. Moreover, suppose we are given a fixed number of clusters $1 \leq K < n$ and respective cluster cardinalities $\kappa_1, \ldots, \kappa_K$. We look for a K-partition $\{C_1, \ldots, C_K\}$ of $\mathbb{N}_n$. For $1 \leq i \leq n$ and $1 \leq k \leq K$ let

$$\xi_{ik} := \begin{cases} 1 & \text{if} \quad i \in C_k \\ 0 & \text{if} \quad i \notin C_k \end{cases}$$

be indicator variables: $\xi_{ik} = 1$ iff object number i belongs to cluster C_k. Further, let $c_1, \ldots, c_K \in \mathbb{R}^m$ denote the centres of gravity, i.e.

$$c_k := \frac{1}{\kappa_k} \sum_{i=1}^{n} x_i \xi_{ik}.$$

We formulate the following **optimization problem** to be solved for the ξ_{ik}:

$$z_9(\mathcal{C}) = \sum_{k_1=1}^{K-1} \sum_{k_2=k_1+1}^{K} \|c_{k_1} - c_{k_2}\|_2^2 \longrightarrow \max$$

s.t.

$$\sum_{k=1}^{K} \xi_{ik} = 1 \quad (i = 1, \ldots, n)$$
$$0 \leq \xi_{ik} \quad (i = 1, \ldots, n; \ k = 1, \ldots, K).$$

Writing

$$\delta_{k_1, k_2} :=^t (\delta_{k_1, k_2; 1}, \ldots, \delta_{k_1, k_2; m}) := c_{k_1} - c_{k_2} \in \mathbb{R}^m$$
$$(1 \leq k_1 < k_2 \leq K)$$

for the vectors of pairwise distance, we may express z_9 as

$$z_9(\mathcal{C}) = \sum_{k_1=1}^{K-1} \sum_{k_2=k_1+1}^{K} \sum_{j=1}^{m} \delta_{k_1, k_2; j}^2.$$

The target function z_9 yields the (unweighted) sum of the mutual distances (measured by the square of the Euclidean norm) between the cluster centres of gravity, and we aim at maximizing this sum.

[BG07] propose an algorithm for solving the optimization problem. z_9 defines a half norm; the algorithm is based upon an approximation of the $K(K-1)$-dimensional Euclidean unit ball by a suitable polytope. This means the Euclidean unit ball can be approximated by the solution set of a system of linear inequalities. In particular, this allows for applying linear programming: One solely has to solve the linear optimization problem corresponding to each of the linear inequalities.

The algorithm – compared to heuristic techniques discussed above – leads to an **absolute** optimum of the target function z, whereas the heuristics usually obtain merely **relative** optima. However, the algorithm requires specifying the cluster cardinalities $\kappa_1, \ldots, \kappa_K$ in advance. In practical applications, these quantities are typically not known to the investigator. A possible way is to estimate these cluster cardinalities by running one of the heuristics beforehand, e.g. the k-means algorithm. Hence, this quadratic optimization model provides a suitable tool particularly for post optimization purposes.

3.5 Selected Problems from Cluster Analysis Regarding Actuarial Applications

In this section, we shall highlight some problems arising from cluster analysis. Although some parts of the following discussion concern clustering techniques in general, we focus on risk theoretical applications and typical problems the actuary is faced with. In particular, we cover

- the choice of variables for the clustering, i.e. the selection of tariff variables in Subsection 3.5.2

- the determination of the number of tariff classes in 3.5.3

- the problem of determining cluster cardinalities in an actuarial context in 3.5.4.

We have chosen this sample of actuarial problems as it is directly linked to cluster analysis. Moreover, the algorithm proposed by [BG04] requires not only the input of the number of clusters, but also the cluster cardinalities, so we cover this topic as well.

As for the choice of the variables – besides the significance of rating variables – the following technical point is to be taken into account: It is necessary to have comparable scales and dimensions of the attributes when they are included in a cluster analysis. Problems may arise from certain standardization procedures or from the treatment of ordinal or nominal characteristics. As far as we are concerned in our own empirical investigation later on, only metric variables are involved, and these variables have the same magnitude. Thus we pass on a presentation of how ordinal and nominal attributes are to be treated and of how variables of different dimension are to be standardized.

3.5.1   Assessing Clustering Solutions

We mention a general point which should be given attention to when interpreting the result of a cluster analysis. Statistical textbooks usually recommend the following: "Interpreting the results from a cluster analysis is often dominated by personal intuition and insight; the investigator has to make sense of the clusters produced," cf. [FIM01]. So each analysis and result has to be evaluated individually. The following aspects may help to assess clustering results.

Clustering a set of data makes sense when the investigator can give meaning to the classes produced. However, cluster analysis generates groups even when there is no structure at all in the data. In this case, further investigation of the generated categories is useless and no meaning should be given to the classes. There are a number of null hypotheses and corresponding tests to answer the question whether or not there is a structure within the data, see [Eve93]. This issue if referred to as *validity* of classification. These tests are carried out rarely, which may be partly due to their absence in statistical software packages.

Another aspect of a particular clustering result is its *stability*, see [Eve93]. Stability can be examined by randomly dividing the data into, say, 2 subsets and perform a cluster analysis for each of these subsets. In case there are indeed patterns in the data, the two clustering solutions should be similar. Further, one also can omit some of the characteristics used for the clustering and compare results: If we first use $m_1 = 10$, say, variables for the cluster analysis, we can use e.g. $m_2 = 8$ of these characteristics, and the clusters should – for real applications – not alter too much.

As far as our applications are concerned, the following idea is useful: Classifying is effective when variables of interest *other* than those considered in the cluster analysis are observed and there are spreads in these variables over the clusters. With respect to actuarial problems this means that the clustering is useful when claim expenditures for different clusters differ significantly from one another. As for the survey of [YSWB01] we have already mentioned the discriminating ability of their clustering approach: Claim frequency and average claim size vary considerably for the risk groups. This suggests that cluster analysis generates a meaningful division of the policy holders indeed.

When we have discussed objectives of insurance premiums we have mentioned that premiums should be *understandable*, i.e. the tariff should be transparent. This requires describing and characterizing typical "members" of the clusters. As pointed out in [YSWB01], the ability to give meaning to the clusters is a very desirable issue. They write:

> One of the limitations [...] is the interpretation and labelling of the clusters [...]. Business managers would prefer clusters to have clearly defined rules that describe them. [...] the superior performance of the clustering approach warrants further research to describe the clusters in terms understandable to the business.

A very quick and simple way to get an idea of the character of clusters is to look at summary statistics like the centres of gravity c_k $(k = 1, \ldots, K)$, i.e. the mean vector of the variables included in the analysis, see [And73]. Since the expressiveness of the means depends upon the dispersion of the variables, their variances can be taken into account as well, see [Bac96]. Moreover, [YSWB03] suggest making use of other data mining techniques such as decision trees or fuzzy logic to interpret the clusters.

We mention an approach to show one example of how the results of a cluster analysis can be made better understandable to business managers: [WH97] combine a clustering tool and a decision tree induction tool and propose the following 3-step-approach, which is applied to insurance risk analysis.

(1) Develop a clustering $\{C_1, \ldots, C_K\}$ of the object set consisting of n entities. As usual, m attributes are considered, thus each object x_i is characterized by a tuple $x_i = (x_{i1} \quad x_{i2} \quad \ldots \quad x_{im})$. In the survey, a motor vehicle insurance portfolio consisting of some 72,000 records is partitioned into 40 clusters.

(2) For each entity record the cluster to which it belongs. This generates tuples

$$(x_{i1} \quad x_{i2} \quad \ldots \quad x_{im} \quad k)$$

with $k \in \{1, \ldots, K\}$. Use supervised learning (e.g. decision trees) to build a symbolic description of the clusters. This yields a set of rules $R := \{r_1, \ldots, r_q\}$ with normally $q \geq K$ – this shows that each cluster is described by several rules. In the terminology of the survey, a "nugget" is a key client group, e.g. a group of high claiming policy holders. A rule is a description of a nugget. For instance, a rule may be given by

If 'age' ≤ 24 and 'address' is urban
and vehicle type $\in \{$utility, sports car$\}$,
then cluster$= 6$.

As for the example, 60 rules are generated.

(3) Evaluate each nugget according to some evaluation function. The goal is to find those nuggets which are particularly important to the task at hand and to find a manageable (small) set of nuggets which may be further investigated by using human resources. In the example, for each nugget the (a) number of claims, (b) claim frequency, (c) total cost and (d) average claim cost are recorded and each nugget is evaluated by some evaluation function. The goal is to identify those nuggets which are target groups of the insurance firm – in other words, to identify those groups having significantly higher claim frequencies and/or average claim cost. Investigating the corresponding descriptions of the nuggets and the associated customers helps to obtain a better understanding of these key groups.

Finally, it is important to investigate another aspect of *validity* of the clustering model. Suppose an insurance portfolio has been classified into various risk categories according to certain risk factors (tariff variables). Possibly, these factors change in time. Therefore, it is necessary to periodically check whether the risk factors are still valid, see [YSWB03]. This leads to the next issue.

3.5.2 Selection of Tariff Variables

Class rating relies on the assumption that the insurer may judge a risk by considering certain a priori known characteristics, the *objective risk factors*, see [Hel74]: The goal is to extract the parameters which significantly determine the causation and the size of claims. By means of risk classification, the insurer may grade the premiums according to the riskiness of given risks according to the values of the risk factors. The first step of each classification system is thus to find variables which best reflect the individual riskiness of a policyholder: Her or his riskiness is determined by *behavioural characteristics* which of course are not even known (and thus not measurable, either). As these factors are de facto unknown, one looks for adequate and measurable observables, the *risk factors* or *tariff variables*. The values of these observables are considered values of homeomorphic functions mapping the actual variables onto the observables, see [Zim80]. Hence the set of tariff variables is "similar" (in the sense of topological equivalence) to the set of the true influencing factors. These observable and measurable characteristics serve as variables for the cluster analysis. Premiums for German car insurance policies are commonly[5] priced using information regarding

(a) sum insured

(b) use of vehicle (private use, taxi, hire car)

(c) type of vehicle

(d) regional class

(e) personal rating of insured (bonus malus, "no-claims-discount"; in fact, this constitutes a *subjective* risk factor known a posteriori)

(f) annual mileage

(g) whether or not the car is garaged

(h) age of policyholder

(i) age of vehicle

(j) whether or not there are other users of the vehicle, and their age

(k) whether or not the policy holder owns her or his residence

(l) whether or not the policy holder lives with an at most 16-year-old child in the same household,

---

[5]Insurers are free to select tariff variables within the framework of legal regulations.

see [GDV08a]. It has to be investigated regularly whether some chosen characteristics are (still) suitable to reflect the riskiness of insureds; as for German insureds in the late 1970's, [Sti80] provides a detailed discussion. Does *gender* represent an appropriate risk factor? This delicate question has been answered "no" by [Sti80]. Though female drivers usually produce (insignificantly) more claims than male drivers, their average claim size is (significantly) below the one of men. Here, this results in only a very small deviation of claims expenditures of women and men. Newer figures suggest that female drivers are less at risk than men (ceteris paribus), cf. [GDV09]: Females show a claims expenditure index of about 75% whereas this index amounts to 100% for men. Similarly, the characteristic *marital status* has been checked by [Sti80]. Married persons turn out to have lower claims expenditures than non-married persons. Moreover, the data suggest that non-married persons need not be distinguished further.

We present only one of the statistical methods of how tariff variables can be determined. As we have already mentioned, the selection of tariff factors is the first stage in the ratemaking process. The very first investigations on the relevance of tariff variables are [Meh62] and [Tro77], the first mentioned paper describes the effects of some risk factors such as age, power driving intensity onto claim frequency and claimsexpenditure without using statistical methods, the second paper makes use of empirical *univariate* regression models to examine the effects of some risk factors onto claim frequency and claim severity.

Following [Lem77], [Lem79] and [ST87] and [KL75], nowadays *multivariate* linear regression models of the kind

$$Y_t = \beta_0 + \sum_{i \in Q} \beta_i x_{ti} + U_t \quad (t = 1, \dots, T)$$

are used to judge the significance of risk factors, where t is an index for the policy holders, the dependent variable Y_t is a claims variable[6], the regressor x_{ti} is the ith possible risk variable under

---

[6]Here we do not consider the case that Y_t is a claim occurence variable, which takes values 0 (zero claim size) and 1 (positive claim size). This

consideration, U_t is a normally distributed error term and Q is a set of risk factors (including a suitable subset $Q^* \subset Q$ of tariff variables). Hence, a regressor selection problem arises. Within this framework, we may consider the test problem

$$H_0 : \beta_i = 0 \quad \text{against} \quad H_1 : \beta_i \neq 0$$

and carry out an ordinary F-test. Particularly the following three possibilities to design a heuristic **selection algorithm** arise:

(a) *Backward selection*: First, we estimate the equation including *all* risk factors; then insignificant variables (according to the F-test) are progressively eliminated. In case there are more than one non-significant variables at some stage of the procedure, we omit that one corresponding to the smallest F-value.

(b) *Forward selection*: First, the variable x_I, say, with the highest simple (empirical) correlation coefficient with the realizations of the claims variable is selected. Applying the F-test, we test the significance of x_I in a univariate linear regression model, where of course the dependent variable is our claims variable Y_t. In case x_I is not significant, none of the variables is considered significant, then the procedure is stopped. Otherwise, select the variable x_{II} with the highest partial correlation coefficient[7] with the dependent variable after having included x_I. Then we test the significance of x_{II} in the corresponding bivariate linear regression model, again applying the F-test. In case x_{II} is not significant, x_I is the only variable considered significant, then the procedure stops. If x_{II} is significant, include the variable x_{III}, say, with the highest partial correlation coefficient with the dependent variable after having included x_I and x_{II}. Continue until there remain only non-significant variables.

---

case is treated in [BDMGLM91] who fit a logistic regression model.
[7]See e.g. [vEGN83] for formulae.

(c) *Stepwise selection*: First, decide which variable is to be included using forward selection, second, decide which variable should be eliminated using backward selection (this only applies iff the corresponding F-value is smaller than the critical value). Then, proceed by selecting another variable by forward selection and eliminating one (if there is any at all) by backward selection, and so forth. Stop when the variable to be eliminated is the one which was just selected.

Before implementing such techniques in practice, it has to be checked whether or not the assumptions regarding linear regression models are fulfilled (e.g. the normal distribution of the error terms, homoscedastic disturbances and linearity). However, even when these requirements are not met, the simplicity and availability of regression methods (due to their implementation in software packages) legitimate carefully using the results of regression analysis as indicators for the relevance of variables, see [vEGN83].

Besides regression analysis, there are a variety of other statistical variable selection techniques. Basically, these methods make use of variance analysis (see [Mac02]), discriminant analysis (see [BN75]) or generalized linear models (GLM's, see e.g. [SC89]).

The applicability of cluster analysis to variable selection

We have already mentioned a technical aspect which has to be taken into account – the variables must be standardized. For instance, if we perform a cluster analysis based on the two variables "driving experience" (measured in 1,000 km) and "age" (measured in years), the outcome of the classification would be determined basically by the values of the first attribute. In such a case, transforming the data by a simple standardization produces relief.

Let us conclude this subsection by developing an heuristic approach of how cluster analysis could be employed in the variable selection process in the context of actuarial problems. Therefore, suppose we are given a certain set of potential risk factors and an insurance collective and we have to select at least one variable. Our suggestion consists of performing clusterings of the collective using different combinations of risk factors. More precisely, the objects entering the cluster analysis are the policy holders, and the obtained classification results (corresponding to various combinations of risk factors) can be judged in terms of claims expenditure: If the claims expenditure among the clusters scatters considerably for a particular combination of risk factors, this combination seems to be selective and thus seems to build up an effective classification system. The assessment can be based on the variance which measures the dispersion of the claims expenditure.

However, there are a variety of possibilities combining risk factors and this procedure may become difficult if too many risk factors are involved: Given a set of $m \in \mathbb{N}$ risk factors at hand, not less than

$$|2^{\{1,\ldots,m\}}| - 1 = 2^m - 1,$$

possibilities exist, 2^A denoting the power set of a set A. For the case of only 5 potential risk factors under consideration, 31 rating systems have to be evaluated. If we would like to select at least 3 out of the given 5 risk factors, there remain

$$\binom{5}{3} + \binom{5}{4} + \binom{5}{5} = 16$$

possible combinations to be investigated.

Basically, this approach is a generalization of a commonly used method carrying out *one*dimensional analyses: [Sti80] computes claims expenditures of individuals having different levels of a given risk factor and judges the effectiveness of that risk factor by the amounts of the appearing differences in claims expenditure among the single groups. Considerable differences argue for the significance of that characteristic. To give a concrete example: For civil servants, the claims expenditure index is about 20 percentage points less than for the rest, which suggests the importance of a rating factor "occupation".

Similarly, [Sam86] judges the effectiveness of a rating factor by a reduction of the used cluster criterion in the context of a one-dimensional analysis, see 4.3.3: Suppose we are given a particular rating factor and cluster policyholders according to their claims cost. A significant reduction (compared to the original value, i.e. without classification) of the target function TWSS indicates the importance of that characteristic.

3.5.3 The Number-of-Classes-Problem

There exists a wide body of literature on the question of how many clusters are suitable for concrete applications. A lot of suggestions have been made to deal with this problem. Basically, these proposals can be divided into

(a) heuristic procedures

(b) testing strategies

(c) model selection techniques,

see [Boc94]. We shall give the most prominent example(s) of each of the mentioned procedures.

As far as **heuristic procedures** are concerned, the *ellbow rule* is a widely used measure to obtain an indication for a (the) suitable number of clusters. To apply the ellbow rule, the cluster criterion is to be plotted against the number k of clusters. Now suppose the data fall into K well separated groups. In this case, we expect cluster criterions like z_1 to fall strongly at first (i.e. for $k < K$). However, when we have $k = K$ clusters and turn to $K + 1$ groups, we do not expect the cluster criterion to fall that strong as for the case $k < K$. Graphically, the plot looks like an ellbow. A plausible number of clusters would be the break point.

Occasionally, one also considers *information measures* to derive the optimal number of clusters. We give a prominent example, see [Dic78] or [HK01]. By combining objects to a particular

96

number k of classes, we give away information regarding their different characteristics. The amount of information which is lost by the clustering can be expressed by

$$I_k = \frac{1}{\sigma_{\mathcal{K}}^2} \sum_{i=1}^{k} \frac{n_i}{n} \sigma_i^2$$

where $\sigma_{\mathcal{K}}^2$ is the sum of all squared distances from the n objects to the centre of the entire data set $\mathcal{K}$, and n_i is the number of objects in class i and σ_i^2 is the sum of the squared distances within cluster i. Apparantly, $I_1 = 0$ and $I_n = 1$; moreover, the inequalities $I_1 \geq I_2 \geq \cdots \geq I_n$ hold. By means of the information loss, we can derive the optimal number of clusters. For instance, one may give a limit of 5% information loss, say, and select the minimum number of clusters corresponding to that limit.

Testing strategies are applied to cluster criterions derived from stochastic cluster models. The most important class of tests are *likelihood ratio tests*. The general procedure is as follows: The null hypothesis $H_0 : k = k_0$ is to be tested against $H_1 : k = k_1$; typically, we have $k_0 < k_1$. The null-hypothesis-model (the one with fewer clusters) ought to be rejected if raising k to k_1 yields a significant increasement of a suitably chosen likelihood function.

Model selection techniques mimimize some suitable model selection criterion like *Akaike's information criterion (AIC)* or *Schwarz' information criterion (SIC)*. For instance, [Sch85] proposes to base the decision on one of the two criteria

$$AIC_k := \sum_{i=1}^{k} n_i \ln \frac{\sigma_i}{n_i} + 4k,$$

and particularly on

$$BIC_k := \sum_{i=1}^{k} n_i \ln \sigma_i n_i + 2k \ln n.$$

Much attention has been paid to the question of determining a (the) suitable number of classes. However, this problem should not be overemphasized for at least two reasons, see [Boc94]:

- From a **theoretical** point of view, the "true number of classes" needs not be well defined. Thus investigating the true number of classes is often artificial from the outset.

  We cite two important observations related to the number of classes in automobile insurance. [Try80] finds for *captive* markets:

  > [...] there is no special reason for a firm to prefer anyone [classification] system, although it may be forced towards a detailed classification system by the threat of competition. The type of number of classes of this system, however, should not depend on the number of insureds, the variability of claims, nor the degree of homogeneity in these classes.

  This analysis applies to captive markets only. Clearly, there are strong incentives for an insurance business to install a classification scheme when we assume competitive markets. Next, [Kro71] does not restrict himself to captive markets and writes:

  > [...] the number of classes [...] is arbitrary and the product of compromise. The number must be [large] enough to reduce intraclass inequities to a minimum, [small] enough to produce credible experience, and of a size such that rates can be applied simply.

- From an **applied** point of view, the "true number of classes" often needs not be known. The question "What is the real number of classes?" is not so important as one is interested in the question "How many classes should be formed for the purpose of our application?". Here, economic considerations may play a predominant role to fix the number of categories: As demonstrated above, class rating in the insurance business serves to construct a simple and applicable tariff system, however, it is obvious that the number of tariff classes cannot be arbitrarily high. A balance has to be found between the gains of further tariff differentation and cost of classification. Although it is tempting for actuaries to find a perfectly differentiated tariff, the cost of classifying policyholders have to be taken into account. The purpose of the clustering is essential and even when the structure of the data is better reflected by a higher number of categories, there may be good reasons to reduce the number of classes. The more clusters, the smaller they become on average. Economically, it can be too expensive to serve these small segments, see also [Hof99].

These considerations suggest asking for **application specific criteria**: As demonstrated, asking for a "true number of classes" does not play the predominant role in actuarial applications. We can be content to fix a number of risk categories and build up a tariff from there. By doing so, the choice of the number of classes in such applications is a "political" issue. For instance, a very simple tariff could differentiate between "high risk", "standard" and "preferred" policy holders. The cost of having more clusters is in gathering information, processing and analysis. Typically, deciding how many classes one is willing to form is subject to the outcome of a cost-benefit analysis. Besides the cost of installing a higher number of segments, one also has to bear in mind that – from a certain point – the more risk classes, the lower their **discriminating ability** tends to be, see also [SWB00].

The choice of a suitable number of classes in an actuarial context is not independent from setting cluster cardinalities: The higher the number of classes, the smaller the number of risks per class tends to be. Particularly as for small collectives, the requirement of a sufficient size (in terms of balance) of all subcollectives may affect the number of risk groups, which then would be bounded above.

3.5.4 Determining Cluster Cardinalities in Actuarial Applications

We have already mentioned the great importance of class rating as the most widely used method in premium setting. Using this way of rate making, similar risks are pooled in the same risk class and charged the same (risk adequate) premium. Usually, the risks of an insurance collective are quite dissimilar, thus such homogeneous subcollectives are to be formed: The **equity principle** requires the premium accurately reflect the expectation of an insured's loss. Generally, risks pooled in the same subcollective should be as similar as possible as they are treated (in terms of premium setting) equally.

Obviously, the *smaller* the subcollectives, the more similar the group members tend to be, hence the more likely is the occurence of the equity principle. In the ideal case – irrespective classification cost – only identical risks (in terms of the values of the risk factors) are to be combined in the same subcollective. Thus the equity principle and its quest for homogeneity let subcollectives tend to be small.

However, *larger* subcollectives allow the occurence of the **group balance concept**, the fundament of insurance, if the premiums have a sufficient safety loading[8]. Moreover, by the organization of large subcollectives, expected claim sizes and other parameters regarding pricing purposes can be estimated more reliably; in other words, the statistical inference is more meaningful, cf. [AS88].

All in all, there is a need to balance these two aspects: (i) on the one hand the equity principle and homogeneity implying small risk groups, and (ii) the occurence of the group balance concept and estimation precision requiring large risk collectives on the other hand, see [YSWB01]. In what follows, we look

---

[8]We stress the importance of accurately priced premiums in order to allow for the group balance concept. For sufficiciently large collectives it can be shown that the ruin probability is 0.5 when the premium equals the expected claim size (i.e. without any saftey loading), see [Alb82].

for a plausible determination of the cluster cardinalities in the light of actuarial considerations. Throughout, let us consider *homogeneous* (sub)collectives only.

Insurance Risk and its Components

For our analysis it is useful to break down the components of insurance risk. We will base this graduation on [AS88] and begin with the following statement for a collective of $\mathcal{A}$-measurable risks $X_1, \ldots, X_n : (\Omega, \mathcal{A}, P) \longrightarrow (\mathbb{R}_+, \mathcal{B}_+)$ with total claim size

$$S_n := \sum_{i=1}^{n} X_i.$$

As usual, k denotes the number of classes and $n = \sum_{i=1}^{k} \kappa_i$ is the size of the collective, where cluster i has cardinality κ_i.

> *Insurance risk* is the hazard that for a certain period the collective claim size S_n exceeds the collective premium $\pi(S_n)$, i.e. the hazard of the occurence of the event $\{S_n > \pi(S_n)\} \in \mathcal{A}$.[9]

In other words, this describes the risk of a ruin. There are two components (reasons) of insurance risk:

(a) *Contingency risk* describes the hazard that the collective claim size exceeds premiums (plus safety capital) in the considered calculation period when the *true* distribution of the collective claim size is known.

(b) The *risk of error* describes the hazard that the collective claim size exceeds premiums (plus safety capital) due to assuming an *invalid* distribution of the collective claim size for the considered calculation period. This component is differentiated further:[10]

---

[9]In a more general setting, safety funds amounting to Z may be included in the analysis, this leads to the event $\{S_n > \pi(S_n) + Z\}$.

[10]To be precise, the following two parts of the risk of error cannot be separated entirely: Each error in the statistical diagnosis affects the prognosis.

- The incomplete information regarding the true claim size distribution may be due to mistakes in the statistical inference of past periods and is referred to as *diagnostic risk.*

- *Forecast risk* or *risk of change* represents the uncertainty that the distribution of the total claim size according to calculations from past periods is not valid for future periods.

Measures for each risk source are available: For instance, contingency risk may be quantified by the (one-periodic) *ruin probability*[11]

$$R(n, \pi, S_n) := P\{S_n > \pi(S_n)\}.$$

Another suitable measure would be the expected loss, given the occurence of a loss

$$E(S_n - \pi(S_n) \mid \{S_n - \pi(S_n) > 0\}),$$

which is a conditional expectation. Table 3.3 shows the occurence of a ruin in the years 2000 and 2001. As for quantifying the other sources of risk, familiar concepts from the theory of statistical inference and forecast theory, respectively, may be used, see [AS88].

In the following paragraphs, we analyze how the size of a collective affects the mentioned sources of risk.

Contingency Risk and the Group Balance Concept

We now put forward an argument justifying *large* collectives. The fundamental idea of insurance is the aggregation of risks to allow for the group balance concept – it is hoped by the insurer that big and small losses compensate each other. The

---

[11]When we include safety funds Z in the analysis, the ruin probability is $P\{S_n > \pi(S_n) + Z\}$.

Year	Contributions in Mio. EUR	Payments in Mio. EUR	Loss ratio in %
2000	12 628.4	13 721.0	108.4
2001	13 244.2	13 555.4	102.5
2002	13 624.1	13 215.4	97.0
2003	13 800.4	12 841.6	93.0
2004	13 909.0	12 781.4	91.9
2005	13 581.3	12 578.6	92.6
2006	13 097.7	12 331.8	94.0
2007	12 805.2	12 406.9	96.9

Table 3.3: Contributions and payments in German third party liability car insurance sector. *Source*: [GDV08c]

following sufficient condition of the weak law of large numbers[12] has long been considered a major reason why insurance works and is referred to as the **production law of the insurance technology**, see [Bue70].

Proposition 3.5.1 *Let* $(X_n)_{n\in\mathbb{N}}$ *be a sequence of random variables such that* $V(X_n) \leq c < \infty$ $(n \in \mathbb{N})$ *and* $cov(X_n, X_m) = 0$ $(|n - m| > n_0)$ *for a certain* $n_0 \in \mathbb{N}$. *Then the sequence* $(X_n)_{n\in\mathbb{N}}$ *obeys the weak law of large numbers.*

Proof. See [Bue70]. ☐

This means that the claims expenditure $\bar{S}_n := n^{-1} S_n$ (in a future time period) can be approximated by a fixed quantity if only the size n of the collective tends to infinity. However, it is shown in [Alb82] that this convergence should not be considered the occurence of the group balance concept.[13] Instead, we use

---

[12] Observe that i.i.d. random variables need not be assumed.

[13] It is shown that there are cases where the shown stabilization of the average claims expenditure has no practical relevance.

the following concept of the balance of a collective according to [Alb82]:

Definition 3.5.2 *A collective of risks $X_1, \ldots, X_n$ obeys the* **group balance concept** *if*

(a) *the one-periodic ruin probability $R(n, \pi, S_n)$ vanishes for increasing n, i.e.*

$$R(n, \pi, S_n) \longrightarrow 0 \quad \text{for} \quad n \longrightarrow \infty$$

or

(b) *the average premium $\frac{\pi(S_n)}{n}$ for a collective member decreases when n increases without causing the ruin probability $R(n, \pi, S_n)$ to exceed a given positive bound, i.e.*

$$\forall \varepsilon \in]0,1] \quad \exists n_0 \in \mathbb{N} \quad \forall n \in \mathbb{N}:$$

$$(n \geq n_0 \Longrightarrow \quad \tfrac{\pi(S_{n+1})}{n+1} < \tfrac{\pi(S_n)}{n} \quad \wedge \quad R(n, \pi, S_n) \leq \varepsilon).$$

In what follows, we utilize the ruin probability to judge the effects of an increasing portfolio size onto the occurence of the group balance concept. Now [Alb82] shows the following:

Proposition 3.5.3 *If the (collective) premium equals $E(S_n) + nc$ $(c > 0)$ and if a law of large numbers applies, the group balance concept (version (a)) occurs.*

Proof. Writing $\bar{S}_n$ for $\frac{S_n}{n}$, we have the following estimate:

$$P\{S_n - E(S_n) > nc\} = P\{\bar{S}_n - E(\bar{S}_n) > c\}$$
$$< P\{|\bar{S}_n - E(\bar{S}_n)| > c\}$$

and hence

$$P\{S_n > E(S_n) + nc\} < P\{|\bar{S}_n - E(\bar{S}_n)| > c\}.$$

By the weak law of large numbers, this yields

$$P\{S_n > E(S_n) + nc\} \longrightarrow 0 \quad \text{for} \quad n \longrightarrow \infty.$$

The meaning of proposition 3.5.3 is that a collective obeys the group balance concept (in the form (a) of definition 3.5.2) if the safety loading increases proportionally with the size n. As for the case of a homogeneous subcollective of independent[14] risks we have thus:

Corollary 3.5.4 *For i.i.d. risks $X_1, \ldots, X_n$ with $E(X_i) =: \mu$, $V(X_i) =: \sigma^2$ and $S_n = \sum_{i=1}^{n} X_i$ and $c > 0$, the following statement holds:*

$$\lim_{n \to \infty} P\{S_n > n(\mu + c)\} = 0.$$

We now come to the question of quantifying the cardinality of homogeneous clusters in the light of actuarial considerations, more precisely, in order to make sure that they are balanced. In fact, the balance of each subcollective is required by legal regulations, see [Sie88]. Our considerations follow [Alb87].

Definition 3.5.5 *A homogeneous collective of n independent risks*
$X_1, \ldots, X_n$ *is* **balanced***, if*

(a) *by charging a constant individual premium π each (homogeneous) increasement of the collective results in a decreasing ruin probability, i.e.*

$$
\begin{aligned}
R(n+1, \pi, S_{n+1}) &= P\left\{\sum_{i=1}^{n+1} X_i > (n+1)\pi\right\} \\
&< P\left\{\sum_{i=1}^{n} X_i > n\pi\right\} = R(n, \pi, S_n)
\end{aligned}
$$

or

---

[14]This implies particularly that a law of large numbers applies.

(b) by holding the level ε of the ruin probability constant each (homogeneous) increasement of the collective results in a decreasement of the average premium, i.e.

$$\frac{\pi_\varepsilon(n+1)}{n+1} < \frac{\pi_\varepsilon(n)}{n}.$$

In the last inequality, π_ε is the (collective) premium according to the percentile principle[15].

Against the background of definition 3.5.5, we ask in what cases balance may be expected.[16] It can be shown straight that for the case of a **normally** distributed collective claim size S_n, the (homogeneous) collective is **always** balanced:

S_n is distributed normally $\implies$ the collective is balanced.

Unfortunately, a real collective usually does not possess a normally distributed claim size, see [Mac02]. Trying to argue with the central limit theorem and the Lindeberg-Levy condition – which mean in our context that a mere increasement of the (homogeneous, independent) collective brings the distribution of the collective claim size closer to a normal distribution, briefly:

increasement of collective

$\implies$ S_n becomes approximately normally distributed

– fails as well in practical applications. Hence we cannot conclude

increasement of collective $\implies$ the collective becomes balanced

for realistic portfolios for the following reason: The best possibility to judge the speed of convergence[17] are inequalities of the

---

[15] See example 2.1.2.

[16] Within the framework of our clustering approach, we deal with *homogeneous* (sub)collectives only.

[17] If we denote the distribution function of S_n by F_n, one typically measures the speed of convergence by the *supremum norm* (defined on the set of real functions) $\|F_n - \Phi\| := \sup\{F_n(x) - \Phi(x) \mid x \in \mathbb{R}\}$ where Φ is the distribution function of the standard normal distribution, see [Bau02]. Another suggestion of measuring the speed of convergence is given by [BHW75].

Berry-Esséen-type. However, results based upon Berry-Esséen-inequalities are valid for arbitrary distributions and (hence) yield sizes n of magnitudes of several tens or even hundreds of thousands risks to ensure balanced portfolios. Even when we restrict ourselves to "realistic" distributions of the (annual) collective claim size, e.g. by assuming a compound Poisson distribution (see [DPP94]), the required number of members of a homogeneous collective is still tremendous, see [Alb87]: 40,000 risks are necessary to balance a portfolio where the individual claim distributions have skewness 20; likewise, one needs 160,000 risks to balance a portfolio consisting of risks with individual skewness 40.

Therefore, other concepts are used to judge the dependence of a (homogeneous) collective's balance from its size n. One way is the *normal power (NP) approximation* for the collective claim size, see [DPP94]. For the case of a compound Poisson distributed collective claim size, [Alb87] derives the following statement regarding the minimum size of a homogeneous collective in order to ensure its balance.

Proposition 3.5.6 (Normal power criterion) *Let s_I denote the skewness[18] of the individual claim size distribution, λ the expected individual claim number and n the size of the collective. If*

$$n \geq \max\left\{\frac{4}{9}s_I^2, \frac{25}{\lambda}\right\},$$

a homogeneous collective is balanced. □

According to the criterion formulated in proposition 3.5.6, we plot some values of the minimum size of balanced homogeneous collectives (see table 3.4). Therefore, we choose $\lambda = 0.1$, i.e. the individuals produce on average one claim in ten years. This seems a plausible assumption in automobile third party liability insurance, where overall claim frequencies of about 10% are

---

[18]The *skewness* of the distribution of a random variable X is defined by
$$s_X := \frac{E\big((X-E(X))^3\big)}{V(X)^{\frac{3}{2}}}.$$

λ	s_I	n
0.1	10	250
0.1	20	250
0.1	30	400
0.1	40	712
0.1	50	1112

Table 3.4: Sizes ensuring balance for homogeneous collectives

typically measured, see [Lem85] or [Sti80]. As for the skewness of the individual claim size distributions, we choose a realistic magnitude of 10-50.

As intermediate result, homogeneous collectives with sizes of more than about **700 risks** ought to be organized in motor insurance in order to ensure the occurence of the group balance concept.

Estimation Risk

Let us now turn to the other sources of insurance risk, namely forecast risk and diagnostic risk, and look at the effects of varying collective sizes n.

Basically, the forecast risk is proportional to n for homogeneous collectives, see [AS88] or [Dic78]. Hence, this militates in favour of *small* collective sizes.

As for the diagnostic risk, one can make the following considerations. Before we formulate them, we need the following fundamental statement to derive an upper bound for the ruin probability.

Proposition 3.5.7 (Cantelli's inequality) *Let S be a random variable whose first two moments exist. For $c > 0$ the following inequality holds:*

$$P\{S \geq E(S) + c\} \leq \frac{V(S)}{c^2 + V(S)}.$$

108

Proof. See [Sch06]. □

Of course, the expression on the left hand side in the above inequality represents the ruin probability. Now the safety level of an insurance firm can be controlled by employing Cantelli's inequality. However, determining premiums by controlling the ruin probability according to Cantelli's inequality requires knowing the mean and variance of the individual claim size distributions, i.e. $E(X)$ and $V(X)$[19], see [Alb84b]. As these quantities usually are not available, they have to be estimated (from historical data) according to

$$\bar{X}_m := \frac{1}{m} \sum_{i=1}^{m} X_i$$

and

$$\widehat{\sigma_m^2} := \frac{1}{m-1} \sum_{i=1}^{m} (X_i - \bar{X}_m)^2,$$

respectively, where m denotes the sample size. Measures for the precision of these estimators are their variances, for instance, which are – by independence – given by

$$V(\bar{X}_m) = \frac{1}{m^2} \sum_{i=1}^{m} V(X_i) = \frac{1}{m} V(X),$$

and

$$V(\widehat{\sigma_m^2}) = \frac{2}{m-1} V(X)^2,$$

respectively. The last formula is only valid for normally distributed sample elements $X_1, \ldots, X_n$. Interpreting the individual claim sizes $X_1, \ldots, X_n$ as an independent sample (of the population of *all* risks having the respective distribution), it becomes obvious that we should organize *large* homogeneous

---

[19] $E(X)$ and $V(X)$ denote the expectation and variance of the (individual) claim size for an arbitrary risk X_i $(i = 1, \ldots, n)$ of the considered homogeneous collective.

collectives in order to reduce the precision of the estimator functions and thus to obtain efficient estimates for the expectation and variance of the individual claim size, see also [AS88].

We conclude this paragraph by emphasizing the importance of being concerned with estimation risk. The variances of the estimator functions have a strong impact onto the occurence of the group balance concept: The higher these variances, the higher the risk of underestimating the true values $E(X)$ and $V(X)$, i.e. the higher the risk of underestimating the theoretically accurate premium. Hence, underestimating the accurate premium massively jeopardizes the occurence of the group balance concept, see [Alb84b].

Concluding remark on choosing cluster cardinalities

The size n of a homogeneous collective influences its balance in a number of ways: If the premium is accurately priced, the organization of large collectives is advantageous in terms of a reduction of contingency and estimation risk. These effects are due to the weak law of large numbers.

However, we have seen that for the treatment of the risk of change and the quest for homogeneity, small collectives are desirable: In practical applications, a small collective tends to be more homogeneous than a larger one, and the extent of the risk of change is proportional to its size. A reduction of its size thus reduces the risk of change and is likely to be more homogeneous, hence more equitable.

We shall not develop a final assessment of all these effects here in order to derive "ideal" cluster sizes. However, once more we mention the link between the cluster cardinalities and the number of tariff classes: The results of the analysis in this subsection contain a reference to the maximum number of tariff classes, as the latter must not be so large that balance is jeopardized and estimates become unreliable due to too low collective sizes.

Chapter 4

Review of Existing (Cross-)Classification Techniques

4.1 Proceeding of Cross-Classification Techniques

Let us suppose the characteristics of an automobile liability insurance tariff (e.g. type and engine power of the vehicle, territory, age of the insured and bonus malus) have been already established. It is then useful to pool such specifications of a risk factor with similar impact onto the claim frequency and severity. This is particularly important when the risk factor has nominal scale. One does not need to pool if the variable under consideration has metric scale and if one can find a functional relationship between the variable and the claims variable(s): [Sti80] finds a linear relationship between "mileage" (independent variable) and "claims expenditure" (dependent variable), with coefficient of determination $R^2 = 0.7$ (however, a possibly even better description would be to choose a non-linear functional relationship in order to model marginally declining claims expenditures). Similarly, [Lem85] estimates the relationship between "power" and "claim frequency" and "severity", and [BDMGLM91] use logistic regression to analyze the probability of having (at least) one claim, choosing vehicle-related characteristics like "cubic capacity" and "power".

Particularly as far as nominal variables are concerned, cluster analysis is the tool to adequately deal with the great multitude of specifications of the risk factors. As an example, take the specification of the risk factor "territory". Clearly, this variable is nominally scaled and has many different specifications; we are thus interested in classes of regions which yield approximately the same values of the claims statistics. This problem is addressed in 4.3.1.

However, also in the case of metric variables, cluster analysis may be used to reveal the structure of the data: When we consider our tariff variable "age", the question arises how to determine tariff classes for this characteristic, see e.g. [vEGN83]. One could choose the age classes "under 17", "18-20", "21-25", "26-35", "36-60", and "over 60". But is this classification "optimal", in other words, should the 28-year-old indeed be grouped together with the 34-year-old insureds? To find an optimal subdivision of the collective regarding the (metric) variable "age", we first define *atomic classes*, these are the smallest classes which we do not wish to be divided further. Our example suggests to choose the age in whole years as atomic classes. Then we analyze the values of the claims variable(s) of all atomic classes and the effects of the fusion of basic classes to larger classes: To obtain a simple tariff, we should group the 28-year-old together with the 34-year-old insureds when these groups show similar values of the claims variable(s) and so forth.

The actuary faces the following basic situation which we describe by considering 2 tariff variables (the case of more than 2 characteristics can be treated analogously): There are (possibly high) numbers of specifications of the two attributes. Let us assume there are I' specifications of the first and J' specifications

	1	2	$\cdots$	j	$\cdots$	J'	marginal
1							
2							
$\vdots$							
i				x_{ij}			$x_{i\cdot}$
$\vdots$							
I'							
marginal				$x_{\cdot j}$			

Table 4.1: Structure of a collective with 2 tariff variables.

of the second characteristic. Given this situation, the collective is naturally being split up in $I' \cdot J'$ atomic cells, see table 4.1. As already mentioned, the decisive quantity is the claims expenditure, here denoted by x along with obvious subscripts.

The general proceeding of cross classifying is to reduce the numbers of specifications to e.g. $I < I'$ and $J < J'$, respectively. This is normally carried out by considering the marginal claims expenditures $x_{i\cdot}$ $(1 \leq i \leq I')$ and $x_{\cdot j}$ $(1 \leq j \leq J')$.

Now let us discuss a problem arising from the existence of more than one risk factor when looking at the marginal claims expenditures as described above. So far, we have considered solely one tariff variable; in practice, however, there are several characteristics. [Mac02] shows that in this case the clustering should be carried out multidimensionally, i.e. the analysis ought to comprise all variables under consideration. To see this, suppose we are given two tariff variables (e.g. "territory" and "use of vehicle") and wish to construct territory classes, i.e. the numerous specifications of the risk factor territory shall be merged (the second risk factor is unaffected in the first instance). Therefore, take a look at table 4.2, comprising (i) number of risks, (ii) total claim size and (iii) claims expenditure; where the latter quantity is essential for premium pricing.

Ignoring "use of vehicle", i.e. just considering the marginal

Territory T Use of vehicle U	commercial	private	Total
Region 1	100,000 143,000,000 1,430	700,000 105,000,000 150	800,000 248,000,000 310
Region 2	600,000 228,000,000 380	200,000 20,000,000 100	800,000 248,000,000 310
Region 3	300,000 153,000,000 510	500,000 95,000,000 190	800,000 248,000,000 310
Region 4	600,000 306,000,000 510	200,000 38,000,000 190	800,000 344,000,000 430
etc.	... ...	... ...	... ...
Total	10 m 4,000,000,000 400	10 m 2,000,000,000 200	20 m 6,000,000,000 300

Table 4.2: A twodimensional example for clustering a collective (cf. [Mac02])

distribution of "territory" (that is the last column "total"), suggests to assign region 1, region 2 and region 3 the same territory class. However, when we include "use of vehicle", due to the significantly different values of claims expenditure in the inside of the table, it is clear that these 3 regions are well different and should not be merged in the same class. Instead, the data suggest mergeing region 3 and region 4. In this example, the different claims expenditures of region 1, 2 and 3 are compensated by a contrarian distribution of the exposure on the specifications of "use of vehicle". For classification procedures, this means the following: Either the classification takes all tariff variables into account, or the consequences of a different distribution of the exposure have to be eliminated, see [Mac02].

4.2 Premium Pricing in the Framework of Cross-Classification

We now introduce major approaches of determining premiums once a collective has been cross-classified. Let us consider a car insurance portfolio and let us suppose that exactly 2 tariff variables have been selected. Further, assume we have already car-

	1	2	$\cdots$	j	$\cdots$	J	relativity
1							
2							
$\vdots$							
i				x_{ij}			u_i
$\vdots$							
I							
relativity				v_j			

Table 4.3: Structure of a twofold cross-classified collective.

ried out a classification step previously and generated I levels of the first and J levels of the second variable. This *cross classification* of the collective yields thus $I \cdot J$ tariff classes, also called *tariff cells*. Table 4.3 visualizes the situation by an adjusted (with claims expenditures instead of frequencies) contingency table.

Risks belonging to the same cell are homogeneous with regard to the risk factors. The aim is to approximate the claims expenditure x_{ij} in the corresponding cell (i, j) by the product $u_i v_j$,

$$x_{ij} \approx u_i v_j,$$

where u_i and v_j are referred to as *relativities* with respect to the rating factors, respectively $((i, j) \in \mathbb{N}_I \times \mathbb{N}_J)$. Due to the in praxi large numbers of rating cells and consequently low numbers of exposures per cell, it does not make sense to apply premium principles to the cells in order to compute future premiums: Some cells might be empty or have only a small number of exposures, hence risk premiums for such cells either cannot be calculated or are not *credible*. For instance, [Ste83] provides the following figures: In industrial fire insurance, some 250,000 risks face some 152 million tariff cells, i.e. there are only 0.002 risks per tariff cell on average. In car insurance, the situation is less dramatic: At that time, some 20 million risks face 2,145

115

tariff cells, i.e. there are on average 9,300 risks in a tariff cell (with considerable variation). In what follows, we shall present the most widely used techniques to determine these relativities. The (pure) premium for cell (i, j) is then given by

$$u_i v_j$$

when we assume a **multiplicative** model or

$$u_i + v_j$$

$((i, j) \in \mathbb{N}_I \times \mathbb{N}_J)$ in the **additive** case. There is a large body of literature discussing advantages and disadvantages of multiplicative and additive forms, e.g. [CF79], [Jee89] or [Boe71]. In general, multiplicative models have become more established.

In the multiplicative case, the relativities are determined up to a constant factor only, i.e. $u_i \cdot c$ and $v_j \cdot c^{-1}$ for $c \neq 0$ yield the same approximations of the relative claims expenditures. Similarly, the relativities in the additive model are determined up to an additive constant only.

This proceeding is motivated by the following aspects.

(a) The whole tariff can be described by only few parameters, namely $I + J$ relativities, whereas there exist as many as $I \cdot J$ cells and premiums. Though there are only $I + J$ relativities, the system allows the tariff to have many shades.

(b) Not only its own claims expenditure affects the premium $\pi_{ij} = u_i v_j$ for class (i, j), but also the claims expenditures of all *adjacent* cells. Here, we define adjacent cells as those cells which comply in at least one (that is in our case of only two rating variables exactly one) rating variable, i.e. *all* cells having level i and *all* cells having level j determine the premium π_{ij}. Thus these pricing models ensure a certain stability of the premiums.

Particularly the second feature is being taken into account when we shall propose a new classification system later on.

Now we take a look at the most widely used techniques.

4.2.1 The Method of Bailey and Simon

The method of Bailey and Simon minimizes the weighted quadratic deviation

$$f(u_1, \ldots, u_I, v_1, \ldots, v_J) = \sum_{i,j} n_{ij} \frac{(u_i v_j - x_{ij})^2}{u_i v_j} \qquad (4.1)$$

where n_{ij} is the number of risks in cell (i,j) and x_{ij} is the relative claims expenditure of that cell, see [BS60] or [Meh64]. The goal is to find positive values u_i $(1 \le i \le I)$ and v_j $(1 \le j \le J)$ which best describe the observed claims expenditures for all cells in the a multiplicative form $x_{ij} \approx u_i v_j$. f is the restricion of a rational function, hence (totally) differentiable. Necessary condition for an extremum is $f'(u_1, \ldots, u_I, v_1, \ldots, v_J) = \nabla f(u_1, \ldots, u_I, v_1, \ldots, v_J) = 0 \in \mathbb{R}^{1 \times (I+J)}$, i.e.

$$u_i = \sqrt{\frac{\sum_j \frac{n_{ij} x_{ij}^2}{y_j}}{\sum_j n_{ij} v_j}} \qquad (1 \le i \le I)$$

$$v_j = \sqrt{\frac{\sum_i \frac{n_{ij} x_{ij}^2}{x_i}}{\sum_i n_{ij} u_i}} \qquad (1 \le j \le J),$$

to be solved by iteration. (Sufficient condition for a minimum in $^t(u_1, \ldots, u_I, v_1, \ldots, v_J)$ is $Hess\, f(u_1, \ldots, u_I, v_1, \ldots, v_J)$ being positive definite.) The method of Bailey and Simon has long been used as the standard approach of premium pricing, some practical aspects for its implementation to the pricing of German insurance firms are described in [Zim80] and [Sti82].

However, it has some important shortcomings: First, – due to the quadratic terms – its solutions are fairly sensitive to outliers, second, it can be shown that the total claim size $\sum_{i,j} n_{ij} x_{ij}$ (for the entire collective) is sytematically overestimated $(\sum_{i,j} n_{ij} u_i v_j \ge \sum_{i,j} n_{ij} x_{ij})$ and finally, it is not based on a stochastic model, see [Mac02]. The overestimation of the total claim size follows by the overestimation of the "marginal" claim sizes $\sum_j n_{ij}x_{ij}$ which are of course estimated by $\sum_j n_{ij}u_iv_j$. We prove the latter observation. On inserting the formula for u_i and applying the Cauchy-Schwarz inequality, we obtain (observe that $n_{ij}x_{ij} \geq 0$ and $n_{ij}v_j \geq 0$)

$$\left(\sum_j n_{ij}u_iv_j\right)^2 = u_i^2\left(\sum_j n_{ij}v_j\right)^2$$

$$= \left(\sum_j \frac{n_{ij}x_{ij}^2}{v_j}\right)\left(\sum_j n_{ij}v_j\right)$$

$$\geq \left(\sum_j n_{ij}x_{ij}\right)^2 \quad (1 \leq i \leq I);$$

the same can be proved for all specifications $1 \leq j \leq J$. All in all, this overestimation of the marginal claim sizes leads to the overestimation of the total claim size $\sum_{i,j} n_{ij}x_{ij}$.

In the context of (4.1), we mention that [Boe71] formulates a slight modification of the method of Bailey and Simon; this approach minimizes the expression

$$\sum_{i,j} n_{ij}\frac{(u_iv_j - x_{ij})^2}{x_{ij}}, \tag{4.2}$$

provided positive claims expenditures.

4.2.2 The Method of Marginal Totals

As mentioned, one of the lacks of the method of Bailey and Simon is the overestimation of the marginal claim sizes. The method of marginal sums removes this bias by requiring[1]

$$\sum_j n_{ij}u_iv_j = \sum_j n_{ij}x_{ij} \quad (1 \leq i \leq I) \tag{4.3}$$

---

[1] Again, we restrict ourselves to the commonly used multiplicative version.

$$\sum_i n_{ij} u_i v_j = \sum_i n_{ij} x_{ij} \quad (1 \le j \le J) \qquad (4.4)$$

for the relativities u_i, v_j. On rearranging, one obtains

$$u_i = \frac{\sum_j n_{ij} x_{ij}}{\sum_j n_{ij} v_j} \quad (1 \le i \le I) \qquad (4.5)$$

and

$$v_j = \frac{\sum_i n_{ij} x_{ij}}{\sum_i n_{ij} u_i} \quad (1 \le j \le J). \qquad (4.6)$$

This method is due to [Bai63] and [Jun68]. Again, the solution is to be found by iteration. Due to its overcoming the overestimation problem mentioned above and probably to its simplicity, the method of marginal totals has been playing a dominant role in practical pricing approaches, too.

4.2.3 The Method of Least Squares

The following least squares approach is proposed by [San80]. Here, the idea is to minimize

$$\sum_{i,j} n_{ij} (u_i v_j - x_{ij})^2, \qquad (4.7)$$

which produces the necessary conditions

$$u_i = \frac{\sum_j n_{ij} x_{ij} v_j}{\sum_j n_{ij} v_j^2} \quad (1 \le i \le I)$$

$$v_j = \frac{\sum_i n_{ij} x_{ij} u_i}{\sum_i n_{ij} u_i^2} \quad (1 \le j \le J),$$

to be solved iteratively.

4.2.4 The Method of "Marginal Averages"

We now present another simple method which has a certain similarity to a new premium pricing approach to be tested in the course of this work. In practice however, the following approach has turned out to produce unsatisfactory solutions, see [WT82] or [Mac02]. As relativities serve the marginal claims expenditures; this leads to

$$u_i = \frac{\sum_j n_{ij} x_{ij}}{\sum_j n_{ij}} \quad (1 \leq i \leq I)$$

$$v_j = \frac{1}{x_K} \frac{\sum_i n_{ij} x_{ij}}{\sum_i n_{ij}} \quad (1 \leq j \leq J)$$

for the multiplicative case, where $x_K := \frac{\sum_{i,j} n_{ij} x_{ij}}{n}$ is the overall claims expenditure; of course, $n_{ij} x_{ij}$ is the claim size corresponding to cell (i, j).

4.2.5 Direct Method

[vENR82] propose the following set of equations to determine the relativities:

$$u_i = \frac{\sum_j n_{ij} \frac{x_{ij}}{v_j}}{\sum_j n_{ij}} \quad (1 \leq i \leq I)$$

$$v_j = \frac{\sum_i n_{ij} \frac{x_{ij}}{u_i}}{\sum_j n_{ij}} \quad (1 \leq j \leq J),$$

again to be solved by iteration. Empirical investigations show that this procedure yields similar relativities as the method of marginal totals, cf. [Mac02].

4.2.6 Generalized Linear Models

Nowadays, Generalized Linear Models (GLM) are used to calculate premiums in cross-classified portfolios. This is to some extent due to the development of adequate software implementations. For an extensive treatment of GLM in motor insurance see [Kru97] and [Wal98]. It is customary to model claim frequency and claim severity separately, cf. [HKT90]: This separation enables us to assume different factors influencing frequency and severity and also to exert different influences of a factor on these figures. Also [WT82] argue for separately estimating severity and frequency if these quantities are (at least approximately) independent since predictive accuracy is expected to improve substantially. We present the use of GLM to price car insurance policies as demonstrated by [BW92].

Let us begin with modelling the **claim frequency** f_{ij} of cell (i,j): Therefore, n_{ij} denotes the number of vehicle years in rating cell (i,j) and the random variable U_{ij} represents the number of claims arising from the n_{ij} units of exposure in cell (i,j). Further, it is assumed that V_{ijk}, the number of claims arising from the kth unit of exposure in cell (i,j), is Poisson distributed. Due to the homogeneity of all exposures belonging to the same cell, the parameter of the Poisson distributions is the same for all exposure units within this cell. Of course, we take f_{ij} for the Poisson parameter, and thus have $E(V_{ijk}) = f_{ij} = V(V_{ijk})$. As $U_{ij} = \sum_{k=1}^{n_{ij}} V_{ijk}$ and when the random variables V_{ijk} are assumed independent, it follows $E(U_{ij}) = n_{ij}f_{ij} = V(U_{ij})$. Moreover, U_{ij} is again Poisson distributed, see [Fis76]. Writing $R_{ij} := \frac{U_{ij}}{n_{ij}}$ for the observed claim frequency in cell (i,j), we obtain $E(R_{ij}) = f_{ij}$ and $V(R_{ij}) = \frac{f_{ij}}{n_{ij}}$. To analyze the relationship between claim frequency and the levels of the two rating factors, we set up the (multiplicative) model

$$f_{ij} = \exp(x_i + y_j) \quad (1 \leq i \leq I, \quad 1 \leq j \leq J).$$

This can be estimated by suitable statistical packages, e.g. GLIM.

Next, we model the **claim severity** m_{ij} of cell (i,j): u_{ij} (now interpreted as element of $\mathbb{N}_0$) denotes the number of claims in cell (i,j) and Z_{ij} denotes the total loss caused by the u_{ij} claims in this cell. Let W_{ijk} be the size of the kth claim in cell (i,j) and let m_{ij} be the mean of W_{ijk} (for all k due to our homogeneity assumption), i.e. $E(W_{ijk}) = m_{ij}$. Assuming further a constant coefficient of variation cv of the claim sizes[2] across the cells (this means that the variance is to be modeled proportional to the squared mean), we obtain $V(W_{ijk}) = cv^2 m_{ij}^2$. As $Z_{ij} = \sum_{k=1}^{n_{ij}} W_{ijk}$ and on assuming independence, we have $E(Z_{ij}) = u_{ij} m_{ij}$ and $V(Z_{ij}) = u_{ij} cv^2 m_{ij}^2$.

Defining $S_{ij} := \frac{Z_{ij}}{u_{ij}}$ as the mean claim size, we get $E(S_{ij}) = m_{ij}$ and $V(S_{ij}) = \frac{cv^2 m_{ij}^2}{u_{ij}}$. To model the claim severity, we set up the (multiplicative) model

$$m_{ij} = \exp(x_i + y_i) \quad (1 \leq i \leq I, \quad 1 \leq j \leq J)$$

and hence find a relationship between the mean claim size and the levels of the rating factors. Again, this model can be fitted using GLIM, for instance.

Finally, the **premium** π_{ij} for cell (i,j) $(1 \leq i \leq I, \quad 1 \leq j \leq J)$ is given by

$$\pi_{ij} = f_{ij} m_{ij},$$

which represents the expected total loss per policy in cell (i,j).

4.3   Cross-Classification and Cluster Analysis

This section gives an overview of how clustering techniques are actually used in actuarial mathematics and reviews the most important papers. There are two seminal papers dealing with the application of clustering methods to actuarial mathematics, namely [Dic78] and [LJL80], the first of which was later extended by [Sch85]. Strikingly, all of the following examples relate to motor insurance.

Nowadays, it is common practice in motor insurance to establish *territory classes* in order to reflect the geographically varying riskiness of drivers, and also to distinguish between car

---

[2]The *coefficient of variation* of W_{ijk} is defined by $cv := \frac{\sigma(W_{ijk})}{E(W_{ijk})}$.

models, the latter has led to introducing the tariff factor *type of vehicle*. These two tariff factors are the classical variables which clustering techniques are applied to, cf. [Rad08].

4.3.1 Territory Classes

The inclusion of territorial impacts in a tariff system and aggregating regions to classes ought to keep an automobile liability insurance tariff simple and workable on the one hand, but also fair (in the sense of the equivalence principle) on the other hand, see [Sch85]. It is well-known that there are considerable regional differences in claims expenditures. In the sense of risk-adequate and competitive premiums, the tariff has to differentiate regionally, it thus makes sense to consider "territory" a risk factor. It is made use of the specific traffic circumstances in a region (number and state of streets, volume of traffic, atmospheric conditions, etc.) and the drivers' ability to cope with these regional conditions in order to construct a tariff system, see [Hel78].[3] Also the types of claims vary from territory to territory: It is often argued that town dwellers cause more accidents than the residents of rural regions, but with less serious damage.

[Dic78] reports on classifiying the 49 (Western) German territories – 31 administrative districts and 18 towns – according to claims expenditure as an example of a onedimensional cluster analysis. The overall claims expenditure of all 49 regions from 1973 to 1975 amounts to 310 DM. The clustering is carried out using an hierarchic agglomerative method, namely Ward's algorithm. As a result, 7 clusters are obtained, containing 1 up to 19 regions and varying in claims expenditure from 264 DM up to 369 DM.

Next, the 49 regions also are classified according to (i) claims frequency and (ii) average claim size as an example of a twodimensional cluster analysis, again using Ward's method. Let us consider briefly the first intermediate level of this hierarchical clustering procedure, i.e. when 2 classes are formed: The

---

[3]When a policyholder causes an accident in a foreign region, the accident is recorded in that region where he or she is resident.

first class comprises 33 regions (all 31 administrative districts and 2 towns being alike administrative districts regarding claims frequency and claims average), the second class comprises the rest, namely 16 towns with more than 300,000 residents each. Thus the analysis is able to discriminate between towns (high claims frequency (index value: 149), low average claims (2,218 DM)) and the other areas (low claims frequency (113), high average claims (2,708 DM)), compared to an overall average of 120 (claim frequency) and 2,611 DM (average claim size), respectively. Here, the final result yields 7 classes, comprising 1 up to 19 regions; the claim characteristics of which range from 105 (claim frequency) and 3,057 DM (average claim size) to 171 and 1,979 DM.

Comparing the onedimensional to the twodimensional approach, though the claims expenditure is the product of claim frequency and average claim size, different clustering results are obtained. This suggests that the variables affecting claim frequency may deviate from the variables affecting the average claim size, see [Hel78].[4]

Seven years later, [Sch85] classifies the German 44 regions, including 16 metropolitan areas and 28 administrative districts, according to the following indicator of the (annual) regional claims expenditures ("regional factor"), defined by

$$R_l := \frac{\sum_{i,j} n_{ijl} x_{ijl}}{\sum_{i,j} n_{ijl} x_{ij\cdot}} \quad (l = 1, \ldots, 44), \qquad (4.8)$$

where n_{ijl} and x_{ijl} denote the number of insurance units and claims expenditure, respectively, in ith power class, jth bonus-malus-class and lth region and

$$x_{ij\cdot} := \frac{\sum_l n_{ijl} x_{ijl}}{\sum_l n_{ijl}}$$

denotes the average (over all regions) claims expenditure of class combination (i, j) in a given year. The construction of R_l takes

---

[4]Additionally, claim frequencies are known to vary substantially in time, whereas the average claim sizes are fairly stable.

particularly the possibility of regionally differing occupations of the power- and bonus-malus-classes into account and has been developed in the framework of the pricing method of Bailey and Simon, see 4.2. This standardization is necessary in order to make sure that the regional differences in claims expenditures are traced back to merely regional (and random) impacts, see [Hel78]; differences between the values of R_l are solely based upon such territorial influences.

Having calculated variable R_l for all regions, the following two-step policy is used:

(a) Generate a preliminary classification using Ward's algorithm.

(b) Post-optimization of the classification obtained in (a) using Friedman and Rubin's exchange algorithm.

By doing so, it is hoped to find a classification coming close to an absolute optimum of the target function. For some reason, the index values R_l as defined in (4.8) were computed using different base quantities for urban and non-urban regions, i.e. they were calculated for the 16 metropolitan areas and the 28 administrative districts in different ways. This requires to treat these two groups separately. The results of the classification of the urban and the non-urban regions can be characterized as follows: The preliminary clustering yields 7 classes for the towns (comprising 1 up to 3 towns) and 9 classes for the non-urban regions (comprising 1 up to 5 regions).[5] Next, taking this clustering result as input for the next stage, Friedman and Rubin's exchange algorithm retains the 7- and 9-classes-solutions and does not change the results obtained by the initial clustering.

Let us mention a distinctive feature of the appoach chosen here: The values R_l are not only determined by the characteristic

---

[5] As for this application, the optimal number of classes is derived from the value of BIC, which is a slight modification of the familiar Akaikes information criteria AIC. Each classification under consideration – i.e. with differing number of classes – is assigned its BIC. Low values of BIC suggest a good fit of the considered model compared to competing models.

properties of region l, but also subject to random events. One tries to minimize the random effects by considering several years (as for this application, the data were gained over the 5-year-period 1974-1978). From this, standard errors of the R_l can be calculated (either by including a time series model[6] or without a model for the time dependency of R_l). These standard errors $\sigma(R_l)$ serve as a measure for the random fluctuations of the R_l and depend upon the number of insurance units $n_{..l}$ in the associated regions. A regression is carried out to model the dependency of the standard error of the indicators $\sigma(R_l)$ from the number of insurance units $n_{..l}$ in region l. A good fit can be obtained by

$$\hat{\sigma}(R_l) = \frac{c}{\sqrt{n_{..l}}} \quad (l = 1, \ldots, 44), \qquad (4.9)$$

where c takes value 111. This analysis has ben carried out in order to take the precision of the values R_l into account: The higher the estimated standard error of R_l, the lower its weight for the clustering procedure. It then follows easily that taking the estimated standard errors according to (4.9) leads to simple and intuitive weights.

Finally, we mention the application of fuzzy clustering techniques to the classification of territories as proposed in [DO95]. The task of grouping towns into rating territories is the same, however, the fuzzy c-means algorithm is applied here. Two clustering approaches are carried out in this investigation: (i) The 350 towns into which Boston is divided for automobile rating purposes are clustered according to various claims expenditure indices and (ii) in order to obtain not only actuarial similarity but also higher geographic contiguity, these towns are clustered according to these claims expenditure indices and geographical proximity. Of course, in the second approach each town needs be assigned (suitably standardized)[7] geographical coordinates beforehand. A noteable aspect of approach (ii) is the

---

[6]The indices R_l seem to follow clear statistical trends for some regions.
[7]For statistical reasons, the town coordinates are divided coordinatewise by the coordinates of the town with the largest coordinates, subsequently, the fourth rout of this ratio is taken to bound the coordinates and thus to make

weighting of the variables: The claims expenditure data and the geographical variables are weighted 50% each; of course, any relative weighting scheme could be employed to reflect the investigator's preference for geographic contiguity.

4.3.2 Type of Vehicle

A slightly different analysis can be carried out for the risk factor "car model". The difference in the analysis to be described now is the following: Here, we do not include a claim variable in the cluster analysis.

[Cam86] analyzes risk premiums of individual car models. Now, the *risk premium* is defined as the ratio

$$\text{risk premium} := \frac{\text{total amount of claims}}{\text{number of normalized insurance years}},$$

where "number of normalized insurance years" is a measure of exposure. "Car model" is a frequently used rating factor in automobile liability insurance. As demonstrated for the rating factor "territory", classes of such car models which are supposed to have similar claims experiences are to be formed. This poses only few problems for common car models and models which have already existed for a few years. However, problems arise when car models are so uncommon or so new that no or only little claim data are available. To come up against this problem, besides (i) the claim statistics for the car model itself and (ii) technical assessment of experts, (iii) claims data of similar car models could be used. The risk premium for the car type in question is modelled as a linear combination of the estimates obtained by these three sources of information.[8]

---

them more comparable in scale to the values of the claims expenditure indices.

[8]The paper is principally concerned with finding appropriate coefficients a, b and c for each component. The risk permium for a certain model is then determined according to $a \cdot$ estimated risk premium from claim statistics for the car model $+ b \cdot$ estimated risk premium from claim statistics for a group of similar models $+ c \cdot$ estimated risk premium from a technical assessment.

We shall restrict ourselves to discussing information source (iii), namely to produce sets of cars comprising similar car models with respect to specific attributes: Power and weight serve to characterize the car types. Using Ward's algorithm and choosing 5 classes, 50 car models are clustered according to power and weight. Now the key questions are, of course, whether or not the clustering produces car classes with different risk premiums and whether or not the risk premiums within a class have similar values. The result is: There are considerable differences in the risk premiums of the 5 classes and – compared to the range of risk premiums of the whole sample – the within-ranges in risk premiums are much smaller. Hence we may conclude that this clustering approach helps differentiating car models regarding risk premiums. We critizize, however, that obviously the characteristics power and weight are highly positively correlated. Moreover, other attributes such as average age of car model, manufacturer, length/breadth, form and engine type characterize car models should be included as well.

4.3.3 Contiguous Clustering Problems

One important feature of cross classification techniques is their relaying to *marginal* claim information. Against this background, the following approach is an interesting amendment to our discussion so far: The classification is based upon claim information in the atomic cells.

We now consider a special case, namely that a claims variable (e.g. cost or frequency) is a **monotonic** function of some metric risk factor (e.g. age). To this end, let us assume the following: The younger drivers, the higher their claim cost, and let us build a tariff consisting of 2, say, age classes. The variable age has lower bound a (for instance, $a = 18$) and upper bound b (for instance, $b = 85$). Let there be n_i policy holders of age i, measured in whole years[9], and let the total claim cost for all policy holders of age i be c_i. We aim to determine the best *cutoff*

---

[9]This means we consider the years atomic classes.

point I between a and b, i.e. the class boundary separating the two age clusters. Again, we stress that the essential underlying assumption is that the claims cost are a *monotonic* function of the risk factor age.[10] In such a case, a plausible approach is to solve the **contiguous clustering problem** (4.10).

$$\sum_{i=a}^{I} n_i \left(\frac{c_i}{n_i} - \frac{\sum_{i=a}^{I} c_i}{\sum_{i=a}^{I} n_i} \right)^2 + \sum_{i=I+1}^{b} n_i \left(\frac{c_i}{n_i} - \frac{\sum_{i=I+1}^{b} c_i}{\sum_{i=I+1}^{b} n_i} \right)^2 \longrightarrow \min_{I}$$

$$(4.10)$$

see [Sam86]. (4.10) is a useful criterion since it minimizes the total sum of (squared) deviations within the 2 classes (referred to as TWSS – total within group sum of squares) in terms of claim experience; the group means are $\frac{\sum_i c_i}{\sum_i n_i}$. Of course, this can be easily extended to creating more than 2 classes, i.e. determination of more than 1 cutoff point. The following optimization problem yields 3 classes and hence 2 cutoff points I, J:

$$\sum_{i=a}^{I} n_i \left(\frac{c_i}{n_i} - \frac{\sum_{i=a}^{I} c_i}{\sum_{i=a}^{I} n_i} \right)^2 + \sum_{i=I+1}^{J} n_i \left(\frac{c_i}{n_i} - \frac{\sum_{i=I+1}^{J} c_i}{\sum_{i=I+1}^{J} n_i} \right)^2$$

$$+ \sum_{i=J+1}^{b} n_i \left(\frac{c_i}{n_i} - \frac{\sum_{i=J+1}^{b} c_i}{\sum_{i=J+1}^{b} n_i} \right)^2 \longrightarrow \min_{I,J}$$

$$(4.11)$$

Also, the ideas outlined here can be generalized in a straight manner to the case of more than one tariff variable:

Suppose therefore the existence of two rating factors A and B, where A has levels a_i ($1 \leq i \leq m$) and B has levels b_j ($1 \leq j \leq n$). If A represents "age", some 60 levels for this factor may exist naturally, and if B represents "level of no-claim-discount", some 20 levels (our atomic classes) may exist. In consequence, there are 1,200 cells, an unmanageably high number. Assume we wish to cross classify the collective into

---

[10]However, [Sti80] finds that young drivers are more at risk than the middle-aged drivers, and elderly people are more at risk as well, measured by the claims expenditure. Thus the claims expenditure is not a monotonic funtion of "age". The example chosen here serves for demonstration purposes.

only four cells, more precisely, into a 2×2-system with 2 only levels per tariff variable.[11] We can describe the cells (in terms of the levels of risk factors) as follows:

- Cell 1: $i = 1, \ldots, I$ and $j = 1, \ldots, J$
- Cell 2: $i = 1, \ldots, I$ and $j = J + 1, \ldots, n$
- Cell 3: $i = I + 1, \ldots, m$ and $j = 1, \ldots, J$
- Cell 4: $i = I + 1, \ldots, m$ and $j = J + 1, \ldots, n$.

Let n_{ij} and c_{ij} denote the number of insureds and their claim cost, respectively, of policy holders with corresponding levels of risk characteristics i and j. We aim to determine cutoff points I (as for variable A) and J (as for variable B) by the following **optimization problem**:

$$
\sum_{i=1}^{I} \sum_{j=1}^{J} n_{ij} \left(\frac{c_{ij}}{n_{ij}} - \frac{\sum_{i=1}^{I} \sum_{j=1}^{J} c_{ij}}{\sum_{i=1}^{I} \sum_{j=1}^{J} n_{ij}} \right)^2
$$

$$
+ \sum_{i=1}^{I} \sum_{j=J+1}^{n} n_{ij} \left(\frac{c_{ij}}{n_{ij}} - \frac{\sum_{i=1}^{I} \sum_{j=J+1}^{n} c_{ij}}{\sum_{i=1}^{I} \sum_{j=J+1}^{n} n_{ij}} \right)^2
$$

$$
+ \sum_{i=I+1}^{m} \sum_{j=1}^{J} n_{ij} \left(\frac{c_{ij}}{n_{ij}} - \frac{\sum_{i=I+1}^{m} \sum_{j=1}^{J} c_{ij}}{\sum_{i=I+1}^{m} \sum_{j=1}^{J} n_{ij}} \right)^2
$$

$$
+ \sum_{i=I+1}^{m} \sum_{j=J+1}^{n} n_{ij} \left(\frac{c_{ij}}{n_{ij}} - \frac{\sum_{i=I+1}^{m} \sum_{j=J+1}^{n} c_{ij}}{\sum_{i=I+1}^{m} \sum_{j=J+1}^{n} n_{ij}} \right)^2
$$

$$
\longrightarrow \min_{I,J} \tag{4.12}
$$

Of course, (4.12) can be generalized to any natural number of rating factors and more than two classes per rating factor.

---

[11]Of course, this can be done by applying (4.11) to both rating factors separately, yielding two classes of A and two classes of B. However, when the rating factors are not independent, so this is not a plausible approach.

[Sam86] illustrates this methodology by clustering the collective of a motor insurance company using the two rating factors "vehicle class" (6 categories) and "driver violation" (8 categories), i.e. we have a confusing 6×8-system[12] of as many as 48 cells. For the data under consideration, installing a 2×2-system, i.e. 4 rating cells, results in a 74.1% reduction of the total within group sum of squares TWSS; similarly, setting up a 4×3-system (12 rating cells) results in a 92.6% reduction of TWSS.

Two aspects deserve to be mentioned here: Typically, the c_{ij}'s are subject to random events to a great extent – and thus should not be the only foundation to base a classification scheme on. By excluding marginal claim information, some important pieces of information – namely the claim behaviour of risks having the same level of a tariff variable – are not being taken into account.

---

[12]In this notation, 6 corresponds to the number of levels of rating factor A, and 8 corresponds to the levels of B.

Chapter 5

Development of a New Classification System

In this chapter, we draw conclusions from our analysis regarding (a) balance procedures in the framework of cross-classification (CC) and (b) credibility theory in the first instance. Further, we discuss major shortcomings of CC systems. Subsequently, we introduce the multidimensional credibility-based algorithm (MC) for classifying insurance collectives. In particular, we show that – under certain conditions – MC generalizes CC and hence offers considerable advantages over CC: We identify CC as a special case of MC.

5.1 Consequences of Our Previous Analysis

We conclude from our considerations in 2.3 and 4.2 the following two – related – aspects:

(a) It is plausible and in many practical applications necessary (if the tariff cells are not or not sufficiently occupied; recall our example of fire insurance with only 0.002 risks per cell on average) to take claim information of "similar" risks into account. In this context, *similarity* means that the risks have a common level of (at least) one tariff variable. For instance, if we are to price the premium for a 38-year-old person operating a 150-kW-car in territory T, claim information of *all* 38-year-old persons and of *all* residents of territory T and of all 150-kW-vehicles should (have to) be taken into account. In other words, we look at suitable supersets of risks and exploit their claim behaviour. This approach ensures a certain balance such that premiums become more stable.

(b) Given certain assumptions, it is optimal (in the sense of estimation accuracy measured by the mean squared error) to price premiums according to credibility models. Again, claim information of a suitable superset of risks is taken into account to end up with – in the framework of the model – optimal estimates regarding claims expenditures.

All in all, one may hope to improve estimates of expected claim sizes by an appropriate inclusion of "collateral" ([Boo89]) risk data. Note that all statements have not been made for the classification stage, but for the **pricing stage** – i.e. the final level – in the premium rating process. These remarks are going to be the starting point for our examination later on where we shall make use of them yet in the **classification stage** of premium pricing.

5.2 Problems Associated with Cross Classification

Existing CC strategies have a variety of significant shortcomings which are to be covered in this section.

First, there is a considerable **problem of mass**. Even if the risk variables have been identified correctly, it is very likely that tariff cells are too small to assume the validity of a law of large numbers. It is even likely that tariff cells are empty. The reason for this observation is the growth of the number of tariff classes which depends upon the number of specifications of the tariff variables. The "explosion" of the number of tariff cells is an inherent feature of CC systems: When we choose 10 categories of the first tariff variable and 20 of the second one, there are already $10 \cdot 20 = 200$ tariff classes. This problem is compounded drastically when more tariff variables are used. This combinatorial argument leaves only few risks per tariff cell (on average). We have already mentioned the illustrative example of fire insurance where we have merely 0.002 risks per tariff cell on average. But then we have to pose the question whether the gained cell claim information is sufficiently credible to build a tariff on it.

Second, there arise **problems of homogeneity** insofar that – essentially – CC is based on a sequence of *one*dimensional clusterings where only marginal claim information is used. This involves a loss of information, namely claim information provided by the atomic cells. Another aspect of the homogeneity problem is the **boundedness of differentation possibilities in a CC system**: The actuary's greatest allurement is to combine only homogeneous risks in the same tariff class. How can homogeneity be improved? Increasing homogeneity means to raise the number of categories per tariff variable or to include an additional tariff variable. In the above example, one could raise the numbers from 10 to 15 and from 20 to 30, say. This yields $15 \cdot 30 = 450$ tariff cells. Similarly, one could include another tariff factor with 10, say, specifications raising the number of tariff cells to $10 \cdot 20 \cdot 10 = 2,000$. This leads to a conflict with the requisite-mass-criteria. However, as we have seen in Chapter 1, it is exactly these two criteria, mass and homogeneity, which call for clustering methods in actuarial mathematics. So we have identified two very important weakpoints of existing CC techniques justifying the quest for alternatives. Finally, we add a more **technical problem** revealing the unflexibility of CC systems. Some given numbers of tariff cells cannot be realized by meaningful subdivisions of a collective using CC. For instance, fixing the number of tariff classes as a prime number implies that the specifications of only one tariff variable can be clustered.

5.3 The Multidimensional Credibility-Based Algorithm (MC)

Having the results of our previous analysis and the shortcomings of CC systems in mind, we now outline the following algorithm presuming the existence of 2 tariff factors with I and J, say, specifications and collective size n. As usual, x_{ij} denotes the claims expenditure in atomic cell $(i, j) \in \mathbb{N}_I \times \mathbb{N}_J$, and the marginal claims expenditures are denoted by x_i. and $x_{\cdot j}$, respectively.

Algorithm 5.3.1 (MC)

(i) Assign risk $1 \leq \nu \leq n$ (belonging to a well-defined atomic cell $(i, j) \in \mathbb{N}_I \times \mathbb{N}_J$) the vector

$$x_\nu := \begin{pmatrix} \gamma_{ij}^2 x_{ij} \\ (1 - \gamma_i) x_{i\cdot} \\ (1 - \gamma_j) x_{\cdot j} \end{pmatrix} \in \mathbb{R}^3$$

with $\gamma_{ij}, \gamma_i, \gamma_j \in [0, 1]$.

(ii) Cluster the set $\{x_\nu \mid \nu \in \mathbb{N}_n\}$.

To simplify the algorithm and to obtain some measure for the necessity of a clustering, we make the following

Remark 5.3.2 *Throughout, we simplify the appearing credibility factors in algorithm 5.3.1 to a constant (i.e. cell-independent) number: $\gamma_{ij} = \gamma_{i\cdot} = \gamma_{\cdot j} =: \gamma \in [0, 1] \quad ((i, j) \in \mathbb{N}_I \times \mathbb{N}_J)$.*

This simplification allows us to interprete γ as **measure of the fulfilment of the conditions of the law of large numbers** regarding the given collective. To see this point, it is illustrative to look at extremal cases: If $\gamma = 0$ and thus the complement of credibility $1 - \gamma = 1$, the atomic cells are not viewed credible at all; we only wish to pay attention to marginal claim information – and have a parallel to CC systems. If however $\gamma = 1$ and the complement of credibility is $1 - \gamma = 0$, there is actually no need to cluster since the atomic cells are viewed entirely credible – there is no reason at all to form larger classes since the law of large numbers is fulfilled anyway.

Besides the creation of this intuitive measure, we shall now further motivate the plausibility of our algorithm. Why does it make sense to choose the proposed vectors? Therefore, we look at the *distance* between two risks ν and ν' belonging to atomic classes (i, j) and (i', j'), respectively, which is given by

$$\langle x_\nu - x_{\nu'}, x_\nu - x_{\nu'} \rangle$$
$$= (\gamma^2 (x_{ij} - x_{i'j'}))^2 + ((1 - \gamma)(x_{i\cdot} - x_{i'\cdot}))^2 + ((1 - \gamma)(x_{\cdot j} - x_{\cdot j'}))^2$$

when we select the squared Euclidean norm on $\mathbb{R}^3$. From this expression we see that the pairwise distances between risks may be regarded as *credibility theoretical difference* of claims expenditures.

By doing so, we take *all* **sources of information** into account, not only *marginal* claim information. As far as cell information x_{ij} is concerned, a credibility theoretical treatment seems to be eligible. These cell values are basically subject to random influences due to their small volume.

Further, no statistical **scaling** problems arise from the chosen vectors since all three coordinates represent monetary amounts of the same quality (claims expenditures).

Having motivated the algorithm and realized the meaning of the emerging vectors in the framework of MC, we now turn to a discussion of its advantages over CC. Compared to CC, MC offers the following benefits:

Most importantly, MC (according to algorithm 5.3.1) generalizes CC under certain conditions. To show this, we particularly assume to deal with *discrete* tariff variables like "age of risk" or some nominal attribute – this is the typical scenario where one wishes to apply a cluster analysis.[1] Hence each of these levels can be assigned a claims expenditure. Additionally, we fix $\gamma = 0$ in algorithm 5.3.1. In the next statement, λ denotes the Borel-Lebesgue measure on $\mathcal{B}$ and d is the metric on $\mathbb{R}$ defined by $(x, y) \mapsto |x - y|$; further, d_2 denotes the Euclidean metric on $\mathbb{R}^2$. We perceive an insurance collective $\mathcal{K}$ as set of n risks, depicted as set of points

$$\mathcal{K} := \left\{ z_1 := \begin{pmatrix} x_1 \\ y_1 \end{pmatrix}, \ldots, z_n := \begin{pmatrix} x_n \\ y_n \end{pmatrix} \right\} \subset \mathbb{R}^2,$$

where x_ν, y_ν denote the claims expenditures with respect to two tariff variables X and Y of risk ν. Clearly, CC means to cluster the sets $p_X(\mathcal{K})$ and $p_Y(\mathcal{K})$ separately, here, $p_X : \mathbb{R}^2 \longrightarrow \mathbb{R}$ denotes the *projection* onto the first coordinate and $p_Y : \mathbb{R}^2 \longrightarrow \mathbb{R}$ is the projection onto the second coordinate. After having carried out these two clusterings, the CC scheme is clearly defined.

Theorem 5.3.3 *We are given two tariff variables X and Y, n risks whose claims expenditures are denoted by $x_1, \ldots, x_n$ and $y_1, \ldots, y_n$, respectively. Further, suppose we are given real numbers $\varepsilon_X, \varepsilon_Y > 0$, k_X intervals $I_1^X, \ldots, I_{k_X}^X \subset \mathbb{R}$ and k_Y intervals $I_1^Y, \ldots, I_{k_Y}^Y \subset \mathbb{R}$ such that*

- $p_X(\mathcal{K}) = \{x_1, \ldots, x_n\} \subset \bigcup_{i=1}^{k_X} I_i^X$
- $\forall i \in \mathbb{N}_{k_X} : \quad I_i^X \cap p_X(\mathcal{K}) \neq \emptyset$
- $\forall i_1, i_2 \in \mathbb{N}_{k_X} \quad \wedge \quad i_1 \neq i_2 : \quad I_{i_1}^X \cap I_{i_2}^X = \emptyset$
- $\forall i \in \mathbb{N}_{k_X} : \quad \lambda(I_i^X) \leq \varepsilon_X$

and

---

[1] Alternatively, we may consider *discretized* variables as well.

- $p_Y(\mathcal{K}) = \{y_1, \ldots, y_n\} \subset \bigcup_{i=1}^{k_Y} I_i^Y$
- $\forall i \in \mathbb{N}_{k_Y} : \quad I_i^Y \cap p_Y(\mathcal{K}) \neq \emptyset$
- $\forall i_1, i_2 \in \mathbb{N}_{k_Y} \quad \wedge \quad i_1 \neq i_2 : \quad I_{i_1}^Y \cap I_{i_2}^Y = \emptyset$
- $\forall i \in \mathbb{N}_{k_Y} : \quad \lambda(I_i^Y) \leq \varepsilon_Y.$

Moreover, let $M_X := \min_{1 \leq i_1 < i_2 \leq k_X} \min_{\substack{x_{i_1} \in I_{i_1}^X \\ x_{i_2} \in I_{i_2}^X}} d(x_{i_1}, x_{i_2})$ *and*
$M_Y := \min_{1 \leq i_1 < i_2 \leq k_Y} \min_{\substack{y_{i_1} \in I_{i_1}^Y \\ y_{i_2} \in I_{i_2}^Y}} d(y_{i_1}, y_{i_2}).$

(i) *Let* $\{C_1^*, \ldots, C_{k_X}^*\}$ *be an optimal clustering of* $p_X(\mathcal{K})$ *(i.e. with respect to attribute* X*). If* $M_X > n\varepsilon_X$*, then*

$$\{C_1^*, \ldots, C_{k_X}^*\} = \{I_1^X \cap p_X(\mathcal{K}), \ldots, I_{k_X}^X \cap p_X(\mathcal{K})\}.$$

An analogous statement holds for attribute Y*.*

(ii) *Let* CC_{ind} *be the clustering "induced" by cross-classification, i.e.*

$$CC_{ind} := \{(I_1^X \times I_1^Y) \cap \mathcal{K}, \ldots, (I_{k_X}^X \times I_{k_Y}^Y) \cap \mathcal{K}\},$$

where $(I_i^X \times I_j^Y) \cap \mathcal{K} \neq \emptyset$ $((i,j) \in \mathbb{N}_{k_X} \times \mathbb{N}_{k_Y})^2$ *and let* $CC^* := \{CC_1^*, \ldots, CC_{k_X \cdot k_Y}^*\}$ *be an optimal clustering of* $\mathcal{K}$ *(i.e. with respect to both attributes). If* $M_X^2 + M_Y^2 > n(\varepsilon_X^2 + \varepsilon_Y^2)$*, then*

$$CC_{ind} = CC^*.$$

Proof.

(i) One possible clustering is defined by $C := \{I_1^X \cap p_X(\mathcal{K}), \ldots, I_{k_X}^X \cap p_X(\mathcal{K})\}$. For the optimum opt_z of the cluster criteria z and the value of z at C, we have

$$opt_z \leq z(C) \leq n\varepsilon_X.$$

---

[2] This additional assumption is necessary to guarantee that CC_{ind} is actually a clustering into $k_X \cdot k_Y$ (and not less) classes.

Any other arbitrary clustering C' has (at least) one cluster C_ι ($\iota \in \mathbb{N}_{k_X}$) such that two points x_{ι_1}, x_{ι_2} from C_ι lie in different intervals $I_1^X, \ldots, I_{k_X}^X$. The value $z(C')$ of the cluster criteria at C' must thus satisfy

$$z(C') \geq d(x_{\iota_1}, c_\iota) + d(x_{\iota_2}, c_\iota) \geq M_X > n\varepsilon_X \geq opt_z$$

where c_ι denotes the cluster centre of C_ι. Hence C must be optimal which proves the claim. The second part of the claim (i.e. with respect to attribute Y) can be proved likewise.

(ii) First of all, the cluster centres $cc_i \in \mathbb{R}^2$ ($i \in \mathbb{N}_{k_X \cdot k_Y}$) of the clusters $(I_1^X \times I_1^Y) \cap \mathcal{K}, \ldots, (I_{k_X}^X \times I_{k_Y}^Y) \cap \mathcal{K}$ belong to the intervals $I_1^X \times I_1^Y, \ldots, I_{k_X}^X \times I_{k_Y}^Y$ since the convex hull of those points belonging to a certain interval also belongs to them. From this we can conclude that for the optimum $opt_{z'}$ of the cluster criteria z' and the value of z' at CC_{ind}, we have

$$opt_{z'} \leq z'(CC_{ind}) \leq n(\varepsilon_X^2 + \varepsilon_Y^2).$$

Any other arbitrary clustering CC' has (at least) one cluster
CC_ι' ($\iota \in \mathbb{N}_{k_X \cdot k_Y}$) such that two points $z_{\iota_1}', z_{\iota_2}'$ of CC_ι' lie in different rectangles $I_1^X \times I_1^Y, \ldots, I_{k_X}^X \times I_{k_Y}^Y$. Thus the value of the cluster criteria z' at CC' obeys

$$z'(CC') \geq d_2(z_{\iota_1}', cc_\iota')^2 + d_2(z_{\iota_2}', cc_\iota')^2$$
$$\geq M_X^2 + M_Y^2 > n(\varepsilon_X^2 + \varepsilon_Y^2) \geq opt_{z'}.$$

Hence CC_{ind} is optimal; this completes the proof.

$\square$

Note that the conditions of statements (i) and (ii) had to be chosen fairly restrictive.

In the following special situation, we show that MC is even equivalent to CC. We just have to fix as many classes as there occur *different* claims expenditure vectors, i.e. $|\mathcal{K}|$ classes, and have to set $\gamma := 0$. Note therefore, we usually have $|\mathcal{K}|$, $|p_X(\mathcal{K})|$, $|p_Y(\mathcal{K})| < n$ (n denotes the number of risks) in practical applications since many risks have the same levels of tariff variables and thus the same claims expenditures.

Remark 5.3.4 *The following two approaches lead to the same ($|\mathcal{K}|$-)partition of $\mathcal{K}$:*

(i) *Application of MC with $|\mathcal{K}|$ tariff classes*

(ii) *Application of CC with $|p_X(\mathcal{K})|$ classes for variable X and $|p_Y(\mathcal{K})|$ classes for variable Y (hence $|p_X(\mathcal{K})| \cdot |p_Y(\mathcal{K})|$ tariff classes).*

The *proof* is obvious: In both cases, each data point has its own cluster. Note – for the characterization of the obtained partitions according to (i) and (ii) – that $|\mathcal{K}| \leq |p_X(\mathcal{K})| \cdot |p_Y(\mathcal{K})|$ for finite $\mathcal{K} \subset \mathbb{R}^2$.

The demonstration of these **theoretical properties** of algorithm 5.3.1 is the core result of this chapter and motivates investigating its empirical properties. The latter shall be carried out in the next chapter.

We also mention some **technical virtues** offered by MC. Obviously, an MC system cannot generate empty tariff classes (clusters). Moreover, the number of tariff classes may be specified to any natural number not higher than n. In particular, the number of tariff classes does not rise exponentially when one wishes to refine the tariff (by including an additional rating factor). So MC improves differentiation possibilities.

Instead of using credibility theoretical *differences* of claims expenditures, we were alternatively concerned with the assignment of *credibility premiums* according to

$$\nu \mapsto \begin{pmatrix} \gamma x_{ij} + (1 - \gamma)x_{i\cdot} \\ \gamma x_{ij} + (1 - \gamma)x_{\cdot j} \end{pmatrix},$$

140

i.e. risk ν in atomic cell (i,j) is assigned a twodimensional credibility premium. Apparently, the same theoretical properties can be derived in the same manner as for the standard MC approach according to algorithm 5.3.1. In our empirical investigations, however, the latter approach performed worse than the standard MC according to algorithm 5.3.1. Thus we are merely concerned with testing algorithm 5.3.1 in the following chapter. Moreover, the results gained there serve as an example that MC yields a different – and probably more risk adequate – partition of a given collective than CC does.

Chapter 6

Empirical Investigation

The aim of our research here is to evaluate the quality of MC (algorithm 5.3.1) empirically. Therefore, we compare its performance to a CC system using data gained from the analysis of military road accidents which occurred in 2007. To this end, we construct a collective which mirrors the set of those members of the Bundeswehr who operated a company car in the considered time period.

6.1   Organization of the Data

6.1.1   Description of the Data Sets

Our raw data consist of two parts:

(1) Information concerning road accidents associated with standard passenger cars operated by the Bundeswehr in January, February, June and July 2007 and (mainly) caused by military staff[1]. These data were provided by ZMK

---

[1] This restriction was made to picture the situation of a third party liability insurance.

(*Zentrale Militärkraftfahrtstelle*), the approval authorities for military vehicles. In the data base of ZMK, information concerning road accidents are collected according to a special form, the notice of accident (*Meldung über den Kraftfahrzeugunfall*).

(2) Further, the structure of the Bundeswehr according to military rank and age, more precisely, the absolute frequencies of all age-rank-tuples is available (valuation date: December 2007). This was provided by BMVg (*Bundesministerium der Verteidigung*).

The data for July serve to evaluate the performance – by means of a prognostive test to be described later – of our model, so that we use solely the data from the three months January, February and June to build up the classification model. In these three months we use for setting up our classification system, there is a total of 169 accidents.

The claims data (1) contain particularly information on:

(a) the age of the driver

(b) the rank of the driver

(c) class in which the estimated claim size falls (3 classes: 1 (0-1,000 Euro), 2 (1,001-5,000 Euro), 3 (more than 5,000 Euro)). Unfortunately, due to internal circumstances regarding acquisition of the claim sizes, the actual claim sizes could not be made available.

Though their quality may be criticized in terms of predictive ability, we have to get along with the two rating factors **age** and military **rank** in our analysis. Other risk characteristics like driving experience, issue date of driving licence and sort of driving licence were provided, however, this applies merely to the set of drivers who had had an accident – no information concerning the set of all drivers could be gathered. This important restriction caused us to exclude these characteristics from the investigation. In general, all techniques and ideas proposed in the course of this work can be applied to more than 2 variables in a straight forward manner.

We now list the specifications of the variables used for the analysis:

(a) *Age*: metric variable with parameter values $18, \ldots, 64$.

(b) *Military rank*: ordinal variable with the 24 specifications Schütze[2]
/Flieger/ Matrose, Gefreiter (G), Obergefreiter (OG), Hauptgefreiter (HG), Stabsgefreiter (SG), Oberstabsgefreiter (OSG), Unteroffizier/ Fahnenjunker/ Maat/Seekadett (U), Stabsunteroffizier/ Obermaat (SU), Feldwebel/ Fähnrich/ Bootsmann/ Fähnrich zur See (F), Oberfeldwebel/ Oberbootsmann (OF), Hauptfeldwebel/ Oberfähnrich/ Hauptbootsmann/ Oberfähnrich zur See (HF), Stabsfeldwebel/ Stabsbootsmann (SF), Oberstabsfeldwebel/ Oberstabsbootsmann (OSF), Leutnant/ Leutnant zur See (L), Oberleutnant/ Oberleutnant zur See (OL), Hauptmann/ Kapitänleutnant (H), Stabshauptmann/ Stabskapitänleutnant (SH), Major/ Korvettenkapitän (M), Oberstleutnant/ Fregattenkapitän (OTL), Oberst/ Kapitän zur See (O), Brigadegeneral/ Flotillenadmiral, Generalmajor/ Konteradmiral, Generalleutnant/ Vizeadmiral, General/ Admiral.[3]

As for the **claim sizes**, randomization by using a simple random number generator programmed in `Java` (see Appendix) seemed to be appropriate. The used function `Math.Random()` yields realizations of an equally distributed (on the interval $[0, 1]$) random variable, hence it is easy to generate random numbers falling in a particular claim size class. As far as class 3 (more than 5,000 Euro) is concerned, we have assumed a maximum claim size of 15,000 Euro.

---

[2] and corresponding ranks in the army
[3] including corresponding ranks in the medical service

Year	Average claim size Euro	Claim frequency #claims per 1,000 vehicles	Claims expenditure Euro per vehicle
1980	1,747	125	218
1990	2,333	108	252
2000	3,439	80	275
2001	3,507	77	270
2002	3,488	76	265
2003	3,496	73	255
2004	3,518	71	250
2005	3,564	69	246
2006	3,526	67	236

Table 6.1: The developing of average claim sizes and claim frequencies in the private car insurance sector. *Source*: [GDV08a], own calculations

This procedure leads to average claim sizes of 2,605 Euro (January), 2,520 Euro (February), 2,453 Euro (June) and 1,334 Euro (July) which may be compared to the average claim sizes in the private car insurance industry (third party liability, standard passenger cars, see table 6.1). In total, we end up with a collective claim size of 428,159 Euro.

6.1.2 Construction of a Suitable Collective

We now come to constructing a suitable set $\mathcal{K}$ of risks which adequately mirrors the military driver corps of the Bundeswehr. Therefore, we take the 169 accidents which occurred in 3 months and multiply this figure by 20, yielding 3,380. Taking $\tilde{n} = 3,380$ as the round size of our collective $\mathcal{K}$, we now have a claim frequency of 5.0% which seems to be justifiable and reasonable for quarterly data (compare this to the empirical results of [Sti82], [Lem85], [YSWB01] who find an annual claim frequency of 10% in motor third party liability insurance). As for the car insurance industry, claim frequencies have been actually decreasing over the past 10 years: For instance, there were 67 accidents per 1,000 cars[4] in 2006, see table 6.1 for more details. Annual numbers of accidents within the Bundeswehr have been increasing

---

[4]This means that the claim frequency - not related to the number of risks but to the number of cars - was only 6.7%.

during the past few years; we shall presume the (quarterly) figure 5.0% as the basis of our considerations. Moreover, one has to realize that our results and statements concerning the **relative** riskiness of particular groups basically remain the same – for either choice of the overall claim frequency. So our choice of a particular value of the collective's claims frequency does not influence the general outcome of the risk classification and hence is not essential.

Next, we determine the composition of $\mathcal{K}$ in terms of the occupation of age-rank-tuples. In the first instance, the highest group of officers, the generals and admirals (Brigadegeneral/ Flotillenadmiral, Generalmajor/ Konteradmiral, Generalleutnant/ Vizeadmiral, General/ Admiral) and also the lowest ranks doing their military basic training (Schütze and corresponding ranks/ Flieger/ Matrose) have to be excluded from the set of all soldiers since these groups themselves do not operate Bundeswehr-vehicles. This leaves 19 specifications of the variable rank and 43 levels of the variable age. Second, we copy the structure of the Bundeswehr apart from the lowest and highest ranks on a set M of size $3,380 - 169 = 3,211$ whereat the occupation of the age-rank-cells of M has been carried out proportionally.

Finally, we form the union $M \cup N = \mathcal{K}$, where N denotes the set of the 169 drivers who had an accident in the mentioned 3 months and thus have a collective with size $\tilde{n} = 3,380$ and the desired properties (reasonable claim frequency and being structured similarly to the set of military drivers). Observe that the construction of $\mathcal{K}$ depends heavily on the assumption that the composition of the military driver corps of the Bundeswehr is similar to the entire armed forces (apart from the mentioned rank groups). Due to losses of precision when Excel rounds the absolute frequencies to integers, we presume a collective size $n := |\mathcal{K}| = 3,375$ from now on. Since in our collective the age levels 18, 62, 63, and 64 are not occupied (this also applies to the claims data in July), we restrict ourselves to the specifications $19, \ldots, 61$.

Since we thus have 43 specifications of the first variable age and 19 levels of the second variable rank, $\mathcal{K}$ has $43 \cdot 19 = 817$

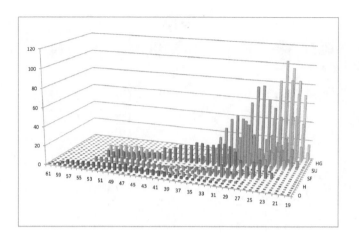

Figure 6.1: Composition of the collective $\mathcal{K}$

"atomic" cells. 513 of these cells, i.e. some 62.79%, are empty. 304, or about 37.21% of the cells are occupied. On average, each cell contains some 4.13 risks. The corresponding variation is high, namely from 0 up to 105 risks. On average, each *occupied* cell contains some 11.10 risks. Fig. 6.1 visualizes the composition of the collective. Fig. 6.2 and 6.3 depict the marginal distributions as for age and rank, respectively.

As already pointed out, the total claim size (sum of all single claim sizes in January, February an June) amounts to 428,159 Euro, leading to a claims expenditure of the entire collective $\mathcal{K}$ of about 126.86 Euro per risk. Table 6.2 lists the important claim statistics. Our Appendix provides the complete data.

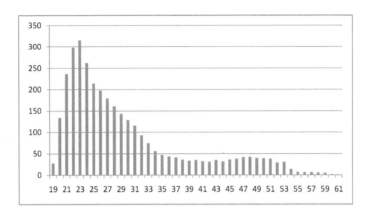

Figure 6.2: The marginal distribution of age

6.2 Risk Analysis

It is plausible that one should not let influence closely related variables the tariff structure. Therefore, one checks whether potential tariff factors are related with each other. To judge the relationship between our two risk factors age and rank, we calculate Spearman's rank correlation coefficient $\rho_{spear}(age, rank)$ since rank has only ordinal scale. In order to obtain a meaningful interpretation, the lowest specification of the variables (19 years for age and G for rank, respectively) is assigned the lowest rank. We obtain

$$\rho_{spear}(age, rank) \approx 0.86$$

which confirms that the relationship "the higher the age, the higher the rank (and v.v.)" is fairly close. We shall come back to this correlation in a moment.

Let us now take a look at the raw data and the riskiness

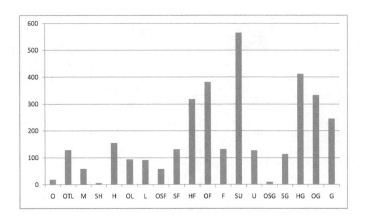

Figure 6.3: The marginal distribution of rank

of some selected subcollectives. We consider the "atomic" cells (risks with given levels of all tariff variables) and the "marginal" groups (risks with a given level of only one tariff variable). Since for these considerations the *absolute* values of the claims expenditure are not important, we occasionally look at the *relative* riskiness of the groups. Therefore, we consider index values here. For any (sub)collective $C \in 2^{\mathcal{K}} \setminus \{\emptyset\}$ we can calculate a **claims-expenditure-index** I according to

$$I_C := 100 \frac{x_C}{x_{\mathcal{K}}} \%$$

where x_C denotes the claims expenditure of group C. Obviously, the index I is constructed in a way such that the total collective $\mathcal{K}$ is assigned the value 100% and expresses the riskiness of subgroup C compared to the riskiness of the entire collective $\mathcal{K}$.

Fig. 6.4 shows that there are massive differences in claims expenditure between drivers of different age – in terms of index

size	3,375 risks
# cells	817
average occupation (all cells)	4.13 risks per cell
average occupation (occupied cells)	11.10 risks per cell
total claim size (Jan, Feb, Jun)	428,159 Euro
claim frequency (Jan, Feb, Jun)	5%
claims expenditure (Jan, Feb, Jun)	126.86 Euro
total claim size (Jul)	57,350 Euro

Table 6.2: Characteristic features of the collective $\mathcal{K}$

values from 0 (e.g. for 32-year-old drivers) up to 257% (for 20-year-old drivers). This means that 20-year-old drivers are about 2.5 times more expensive than the average. Similarly, fig. 6.5 reveals that also the military rank has a high risk differentiating ability. For instance, OSG and L have an index of 0, whereas M have 243%.

In view of these ranges (0–257% for age and 0–243% for rank), the two risk factors seem to have a comparable risk differentiating quality.[5] Moreover, this ability is fairly distinct.

Finally, fig. 6.6 plots the index values of claims expenditure of all age-rank-combinations. Huge differences occur here as well – the most expensive group are the 47-year-old majors with index value 1,896%, followed by the 43-year-old majors with index value 1,774%. Apparently, joint consideration of the characteristics compounds their risk differentiating quality.[6]

In the light of the considerable correlation between our characteristics, it seems appropiate to discuss possible redundancies. Therefore, one could carry out an analysis of variance (see our discussion of statistical techniques to select tariff variables) in order to check whether both risk variables are significant for

---

[5]This is consistent to the found value of the rank correlation coefficient.
[6]This is not surprising since the collective in the twodimensional case is partitioned much finer than in the onedimensional cases, so these fluctuations are likely to be higher.

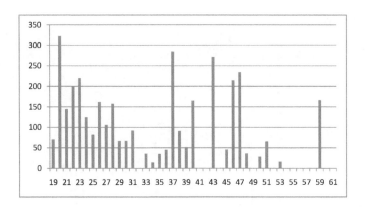

Figure 6.4: Marginal claims expenditures regarding age

the claims expenditure. In this context, the latter quantity (or claim frequency, alternatively) would be the dependent variable, and age and rank would be independent variables. Regression analysis is less appropriate since we have only ordinary scale for the variable "rank". However, we use another intuitive way here.

First, let us check whether the variable rank keeps its risk differentiating property for different levels of age. Therefore, we choose the following example: Fix the two specifications of rank HG and F and plot the claims expenditure index for varying age levels. As many of the corresponding cells with $age < 22$ and $age > 26$ are not (sufficiently) occupied, we shall restrict ourselves to the age levels 22-26.

Obviously, the variable rank does not lose its risk predictive quality – F seem to be less risky (in terms of claims expenditure) than HG even when we base our view on the same age groups.

The other way round, let us take a look at the risk differentiating ability of the variable age. Therefore, we fix e.g. 2 levels

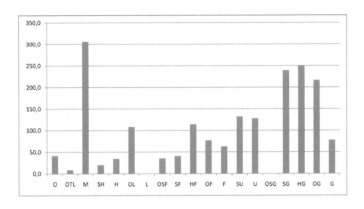

Figure 6.5: Marginal claims expenditures regarding rank

of age (here: 26 and 31) and consider the claims expenditure index for ranks OF, F, SU. This restriction is appropriate since the corresponding cells with rank higher than OF or lower than SU are not (sufficiently) occupied for the considered age levels.

Apparently, the variable age keeps its risk differentiating ability, even when we consider the same ranks: The 22-year-old drivers have index values not higher than the 27-year-old drivers.

The following remark should be added to the previous investigation concerning redundancies: We have selected such examples which allow to show the described effects in a manifest way. Also we have picked other examples, some of them did not reveal such effects, but showed unclear and diffuse developings of index values.

All in all, it is reasonable to consider both age and military rank for our subsequent analysis. Further information (better

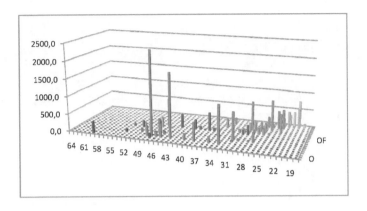

Figure 6.6: Claims expenditures regarding age and rank

description) of the risks can be achieved without emerging additional classification cost – the data are availabe anyway – hence both characteristics should be included. Possibly, the variable rank reflects the mentality of the drivers and their driving behaviour better than age does.

6.3 Application of the Multidimensional Credibility-Based Algorithm

We are now ready to test algorithm 5.3.1 for varying values of the credibility factor γ empirically. Two points deserve to be mentioned in advance: First, we use the software package ClustanGraphics for cluster analysis. Second, we choose target function z_1 and use the k-means algorithm in order to cluster. The set to be clustered can be depicted by scatter plot 6.9.

Table 6.3 characterizes the clusters by the most important

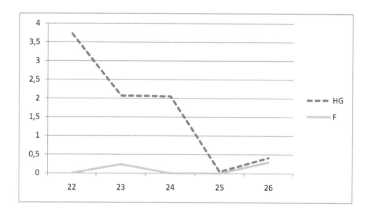

Figure 6.7: Index values of HG and F for risks aged 22-26 years

data. It turns out each choice of $\gamma \in \{0.05, 0.1, 0.2\}$ leads to to the same partition of the collective.

We are now interested in the empirical performance of MC. Before we judge it by means of some criteria, we provide an overview given by table 6.4. As already mentioned, there are 43 military drivers who had an accident in July 2007, leading to total claim size 57,350 Euro. Table 6.4 lists the predicted and observed claims expenditures for July. As for the predicted premium $\hat{\pi}$, we take a third of the corresponding value listed in table 6.3 since we come from 3-month-data and wish to predict one-month-data, i.e.

$$\hat{\pi}_C = 3^{-1} x_C$$

where x_C denotes the claims expenditure of cluster C as stated in table 6.3.[7] Of course, this is only a simple (though plausible)

---

[7]We shall differentiate between the terms "claims expenditure" and "premium" though their values are equal as for MC. However, claims expenditures and premiums in a CC setting normally do not coincide.

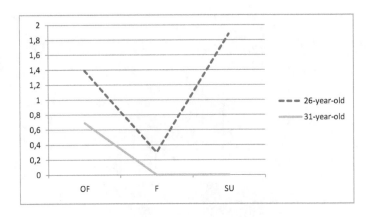

Figure 6.8: Index values of 26- and 31-year-old risks with ranks OF, F and SU

choice; in a more general setting, one might want to take seasonal effects into account. Apparently, there are strong seasonal effects within the data: We reckon to obtain $3^{-1} \cdot 428,159 \approx 142,720$ Euro total claim size for July, but only 57,350 Euro are actually observed. Possibly, seasonal influences are also reflected by the values of average claim sizes: Recall we have roughly 2,500 Euro for January, February and June and only some 1,300 Euro for July.

The following example illustrates necessary calculations.

Example 6.3.1 Let us take a look at cluster 3 containing 858 risks. According to our results listed in table 6.3, we predict $\hat{\pi}_1 = 3^{-1} \cdot 210.92 \approx 70.31$ Euro claims expenditure for July. The actually observed total claim size as for cluster 3 in July amounts to 30,239 Euro. Hence the observed premium amounts to $\pi_1 = \frac{30,239}{858} \approx 35.24$ Euro. The (absolute) error is thus given

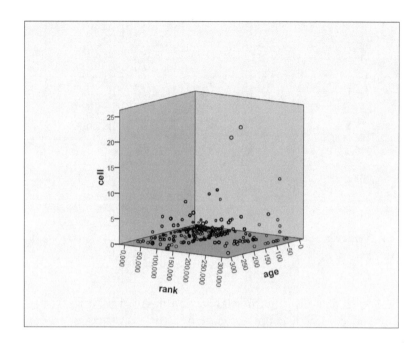

Figure 6.9: Graphical representation of the collective (with $\gamma = 0.1$)

by $R_1 := \hat{\pi}_1 - \pi_1 \approx 35.06$ Euro which amounts to a relative error (related to the predicted premium) of $r_1 := \frac{R_1}{\hat{\pi}_1} \approx 49.87\%$.

6.4 Application of Cross-Classification

In this section, we apply a CC system to compare its outcome with the one of MC. Therefore, two methods are introduced in the first instance, one of which is actually selected. Throughout, we long for classifications based on **claims expenditure** – as usual in the insurance industry. To describe them precisely, the following notation is used: x_{ij} denotes the claims expenditure in atomic cell (i, j), where i is the level of age and j is the level of rank. The marginal claims expenditure of age level i is denoted

Cluster	Size	Total claim size Euro	X Euro	I %
1	294	4,418	15.03	11.85
2	460	75,174	163.42	128.82
3	858	180,972	210.92	166.26
4	196	22,092	112.71	88.85
5	619	62,232	100.54	79.25
6	182	7,126	39.15	30.86
7	177	59,803	337.87	266.33
8	38	0	0.00	0.00
9	82	621	7.57	5.97
10	68	114	1.68	1.32
11	261	15,219	58.31	45.96
12	140	388	2.77	2.18
Sum	3,375	428,159	–	–

Table 6.3: Claim statistics of the clusters according to algorithm 5.3.1 – data basis: January, February and June

by $x_{i.}$ and the marginal claims expenditure of rank j is denoted by $x_{.j}$. Using this notation, we are now ready to formulate CC techniques.

(1) Consider solely the *marginal* claims expenditures for each variable. Therefore, characterize risk ν in cell (i, j) by $x_\nu := x_{i.} \in \mathbb{R}$ to form age classes. Analogously, assign risk ν in cell (i, j) the vector $x_\nu := x_{.j} \in \mathbb{R}$ to obtain rank classes.

(2) Consider the *cell* claims expenditures as motivated in Chapter 5 and assign risk ν belonging to cell (i, j) the vector ${}^t(x_{i1}, \ldots, x_{i,19}) \in \mathbb{R}^{19}$ to generate age classes. Similarly, characterize risk ν belonging to cell (i, j) by $x_\nu := {}^t (x_{19,j}, \ldots, x_{64,j}) \in \mathbb{R}^{43}$ to form rank classes.

In either case, the set $\{x_\nu \mid \nu = 1, \ldots, n\}$ is to be clustered.

Cluster	Total claim size Euro	π Euro	$\hat{\pi}$ Euro	Absolute error Euro	Relative error %
1	3,265	11.11	5.01	-6.10	-121.71
2	8,025	17.45	54.47	37.03	67.97
3	30,239	35.24	70.31	35.06	49.87
4	3,023	15.42	37.57	22.15	58.95
5	2,906	4.69	33.51	28.82	85.99
6	699	3.84	13.05	9.21	70.57
7	6,517	36.82	112.62	-17.33	67.31
8	0	0.00	0.00	0.00	–
9	516	6.29	2.52	-3.77	-149.28
10	299	4.40	0.56	-3.84	-686.84
11	1,365	5.23	19.44	14.21	73.09
12	496	3.54	0.92	-2.62	-283.51
Sum	57,350	–	–	–	–

Table 6.4: Algorithm 5.3.1 (MC). Forecasted vs. actually observed premiums – data basis: July

Cluster	Members	Size	Total claim size Euro
1	32-36, 41, 42, 44, 45, 48-50, 52-58, 60, 61	662	11,793
2	20, 22, 23, 37, 43, 46, 47, 59	905	211,895
3	19, 25, 27, 29-31, 38, 39, 51	917	74,543
4	21, 24, 26, 28, 40	891	129,928
Sum	–	3,375	428,159

Table 6.5: Classification result regarding "age"

We restrict ourselves to the application of method (1) since we claim that the cell values x_{ij} needed for applying method (2) in real world databases are not credible enough to base any classification scheme on them. It is exactly the conjecture that these cell values are not suitable to indicate the degree of riskiness which causes us to cluster. Due to their (normally) small sizes, they are considered strongly influenced by random events.

As figures 6.4 and 6.5 suggest, it is plausible to choose 3 clusters for "military rank" and e.g. 4 clusters for "age".

Age classes

So let us choose 4 age categories. Table 6.5 shows the 4 age classes together with their claims expenditure.

As we will see in a moment, this segmentation is less inter-

Cluster	Members	Size	Total claim size Euro
1	M, SG, HG, OG	914	220,056
2	OL, HF, OF, SU, U, G	1,733	185,328
3	O, OTL, SH, H, L, OSF, SF, F, OSG	728	22,775
Sum	–	3,375	428,159

Table 6.6: Classification result regarding "military rank"

pretable than the one for the ranks. Anyway, the differences between the clusters are notable: The claims expenditure of cluster 1 amounts to only 14% of the overall claims expenditure; for cluster 2 this figure is 185%.

Rank classes

As pointed out, it is plausible to form 3 rank categories. Table 6.6 shows the composition of the 3 clusters together with their claims expenditures.

This reveals a very intuitive pattern in the data: Note that the found segmentation mirrors the natural rank structure of $\mathcal{K}$: Cluster 1 contains mainly ranks belonging to the rank group "Mannschaften" (grave risks), cluster 2 (medium risks) consists mainly of "Unteroffiziere", and cluster 3 represents mainly "Offiziere" (good risks).

The structure of the cross-classified collective

Table 6.7 depicts the structure of $\mathcal{K}$ according to the obtained rank and age classes. Our cross classification yields a 4×3-system of 12 tariff cells.

To determine the premium $\hat{\pi}_{ij}$ for tariff cell $(i,j) \in \mathbb{N}_4 \times \mathbb{N}_3$), we apply the method of Simon and Bailey. Therefore, we minimize the function $f : \mathbb{R}_+^7 \longrightarrow \mathbb{R}$,

$$
{}^t(u_1, \ldots, u_4, v_1, \ldots, v_3) \mapsto \sum_{i=1}^{4} \sum_{j=1}^{3} n_{ij} \frac{(x_{ij} - u_i v_j x_{\mathcal{K}})^2}{u_i v_j x_{\mathcal{K}}}
$$

	Rank class 1	Rank class 2	Rank class 3	marginal
Age class 1	27 4,677 173.22	299 4,418 14.78	336 2,698 8.03	662 11,793 17.81
Age class 2	443 134,570 303.77	334 67,991 203.57	128 9,334 72.92	905 211,895 234.14
Age class 3	130 6,760 52.00	619 62,232 100.54	168 5,551 33.04	917 74,543 81.29
Age class 4	314 74,049 235.82	481 50,687 105.38	96 5,192 54.08	891 129,928 145.82
marginal	914 220,056 240.59	1,733 185,328 106.94	728 22,775 31.28	3,375 428,159 126.86

Table 6.7: Structure of the cross-classified collective (first entry: exposure, second entry: claim size, third entry: claims expenditure)

	Rank class 1	Rank class 2	Rank class 3	relativity
Age class 1	60.53	35.99	13.24	$u_1 \approx 0.289$
Age class 2	316.82	188.38	69.28	$u_2 \approx 1.512$
Age class 3	148.08	88.05	32.38	$u_3 \approx 0.707$
Age class 4	211.40	125.70	46.23	$u_4 \approx 1.009$
relativity	$v_1 \approx 1.652$	$v_2 \approx 0.982$	$v_3 \approx 0.361$	–

Table 6.8: Premiums according to the method of Simon and Bailey – data basis: January, February and June

using `Mathematica 6`. $u_1, \ldots, u_4$ are the relativities with respect to "age" and $v_1, \ldots, v_3$ are the marginal factors regarding "rank", n_{ij} and x_{ij} denote the number of risks and claims expenditure, respectively, in tariff cell (i, j) and $x_{\mathcal{K}} = 126.86$ is the overall claims expenditure. Table 6.8 summarizes the results. Of course, the (fitted) premium for tariff cell (i, j) is given by $x_{\mathcal{K}} u_i v_j \approx 126.86 u_i v_j$.

Empirical performance

We now examine the performance of the CC system by means of a prognostic test. Of course, the forecasted premium for the

Cell	Total claim size Euro	π Euro	$\hat{\pi}$ Euro	Absolute error Euro	Relative error %
(1,1)	0	0	20.18	20.18	100
(1,2)	3,265	10.92	12.00	1.08	9.00
(1,3)	1,175	3.50	4.41	0.91	20.63
(2,1)	17,036	38.37	105.61	67.24	63.67
(2,2)	5,748	17.21	62.79	45.58	72.60
(2,3)	2,047	16.51	23.09	6.58	28.51
(3,1)	3,732	28.71	49.36	20.65	41.84
(3,2)	2,906	4.69	29.35	24.66	84.02
(3,3)	319	1.90	10.79	8.89	82.42
(4,1)	15,988	50.92	70.47	19.55	27.74
(4,2)	3,741	7.78	41.90	34.12	81.43
(4,3)	1,393	13.93	15.41	1.48	9.60
Sum	57,350	–	–	–	–

Table 6.9: Cross-classification (CC). Forecasted vs. actually observed premiums – data basis: July

one-month-period July and triff cell (i,j) is given by $3^{-1} x_{\mathcal{K}} u_i v_j$. To illustrate the procedure, we give the following

Example 6.4.1 There are 299 risks in tariff cell (1,2), one of which produces a claim in July with claim size 3,265 Euro. Thus the observed risk premium is $\pi_{(1,2)} = \frac{3,265}{299} \approx 10.92$ Euro. Our forecast is $\hat{\pi}_{(1,2)} \approx 3^{-1} \cdot 126.86 \cdot 0.2889 \cdot 0.9821 \approx 12.00$. The error is thus $12.00 - 10.92 = 1.08$ Euro or 9% (with respect to the predicted value), respectively.

Table 6.9 summarizes our results.

6.5 Economic Evaluation

6.5.1 Criteria

To evaluate the performance of the considered tariff systems economically, we carry out a *prognostic test*. Therefore, **predicted** premiums are compared to **actually observed** premiums. In this subsection, we introduce the most frequently used model evaluation criteria. Within this context, it is common to focus on the following fundamental principles as mentioned in [BS60]. Each tariff ought to

(a) be actuarially balanced

(b) reflect the relative credibility of cells

(c) provide a minimal amount of departure from the raw data for the maximum number of people

(d) fit cell data so that deviations of the fitted values from the experience are due only to chance.

As for (a), it turns out that the application of MC yields four unbalanced risk classes: Clusters 1, 9, 10 and 12 show higher observed claims than charged premiums. Clearly, applying MC obeys property (b) – as for the balance aspect note that we take the claims expenditure as the premium. Attributes (c) and (d) are just model-fitting criteria which we shall evaluate by meaningful measures to be proposed in the following. According to [Boe71], not only one but several criteria ought to be used to compare performances of certain tariffs. In what follows, k denotes the number of tariff classes, $\hat{\pi}$ and π are predicted and actually observed, respectively, premiums.

The **balance** of a collective can be assessed by

$$crit_1 := \frac{\sum_{i=1}^{k} \kappa_i \hat{\pi}_i}{\sum_{i=1}^{k} \kappa_i \pi_i}, \tag{6.1}$$

the ratio between estimated and observed total claim sizes, see [Ajn86] and [Boe71]. Obviously, if $crit_1$ is not less than (but – due to competitive markets – hopefully close to) 1, the tariff is empirically balanced: The revenues $\sum_{i=1}^{k} \kappa_i \hat{\pi}_i$ exceed the observed claim cost $\sum_{i=1}^{k} \kappa_i \pi_i$. The relevance of this criteria is drastically illustrated by the situation of German car insurers in the five years from 2004 until 2008: Only 32 out of 78 firms under consideration were able to earn money due to their underwriting business, see [Völ08]. Alternatively, [Boe71] proposes the (unweighted) average difference between estimated and forecasted values; we formulate a weighted version of his criteria

$$crit_2 := \sum_{i=1}^{k} \frac{\kappa_i}{n} (\hat{\pi}_i - \pi_i). \tag{6.2}$$

As the appearing differences can be positive or negative (or null), the latter criteria gives information about whether and how well these differences compensate each other or whether there is a systematic deviation in a certain direction. Obviously, small absolute values of this figure indicate a balanced tariff.

Next, we look at criteria describing the **goodness of fit**. The most commonly used measures for predictive accuracy are the *(observed) mean squared error*

$$MSE := \sum_{i=1}^{k} \frac{\kappa_i}{n} (\hat{\pi}_i - \pi_i)^2, \tag{6.3}$$

the *(observed) root mean squared error*

$$crit_3 := \sqrt{MSE} \tag{6.4}$$

and the *(observed) mean absolute error*

$$crit_4 := MAE := \sum_{i=1}^{k} \frac{\kappa_i}{n} |\hat{\pi}_i - \pi_i|, \tag{6.5}$$

see [CF79], [FTW81], [WTC84], [Jee89], [YSWB01] and [YSWB03]. As the root is strictly monotonic increasing, $crit_3(A) < crit_3(B)$ for particular models A and B iff $MSE(A) < MSE(B)$. These criteria are based upon differences between forecasted and actually observed premiums, where the premiums are weighted according to cluster cardinalities. Clearly, these figures are non-negative. Low values of these criteria indicate a preferable tariff. The MSE puts greater weights on large errors than the MAE does.

Further, [Boe71] suggests the following quantity resembling the χ^2-test of goodness of fit

$$crit_5 := \sum_{i=1}^{k} \frac{\kappa_i (\hat{\pi}_i - \pi_i)^2}{\hat{\pi}_i} \tag{6.6}$$

provided $\hat{\pi}_i \neq 0$ $(1 \leq i \leq k)$. Again, differences between predicted and observed premiums are the basis of this measure.

Its similarity to the criterion of Bailey and Simon is obvious. Again, low values of this figure indicate a good tariff.

Also the (weighted and unweighted version of the) *empirical correlation coefficient* between observed and estimated class premiums

$$crit_6 := \rho(\pi, \hat{\pi}) \qquad (6.7)$$

is proposed, see [Boe71] and [CF79]. Obviously, good tariffs correspond to high values (i.e. close to 1) of the correlation coefficient. Alternatively, the squared correlation coefficient is used. In the literature, it is common to compute both exposure-weighted and unweighted correlation coefficients.

Finally, besides our *balance* and *goodness of fit* considerations, one can look at – as we would like to call them – **"benefits of classification"** (compared to a situation without classification). For instance, such an intuitive measure is the *variance reduction* – relative to the situation with a "flat rate", i.e. all risks pay the same premium being equal to the overall claims expenditure $\hat{\pi}_{\mathcal{K}} = \frac{\sum_{i=1}^{k} \kappa_i x_i}{n}$ (x_i denotes the claims expenditure of tariff class i in the *current* period) –

$$crit_7 := \frac{\sum_{i=1}^{k} \kappa_i (\pi_i - \hat{\pi}_{\mathcal{K}})^2 - \kappa_i (\pi_i - \hat{\pi}_i)^2}{\sum_{i=1}^{k} \kappa_i (\pi_i - \hat{\pi}_{\mathcal{K}})^2}$$
$$= 1 - \frac{\sum_{i=1}^{k} \kappa_i (\pi_i - \hat{\pi}_i)^2}{\sum_{i=1}^{k} \kappa_i (\pi_i - \hat{\pi}_{\mathcal{K}})^2} \qquad (6.8)$$

cf. [Ajn86]. In the latter formula, π_i stands for the observed claims expenditure of tariff class i in the *next* period. This figure mirrors the benefit of grading premiums compared to the structure with a uniform premium (flat rate) for all risks. Obviously, high values of $crit_7$ indicate a good tariff.

Table 6.10 summarizes optimal criteria values.

6.5.2 Calculations

We examine the goodness of the discussed classification schemes by comparing some of the above mentioned measures. Particu-

criteria	$crit_1$	$crit_2$	$crit_3$	$crit_4$	$crit_5$	$crit_6$	$crit_7$
optimal value	1	0	0	0	0	1	1

Table 6.10: Optimal values for the proposed criteria

	$crit_1$	$crit_2$	$crit_3$	$crit_4$	$crit_5$	$crit_6$	$crit_7$
(1) CC (no balancing)	2.49	85,371	33.82	27.40	65K	0.62	-28.85%
(2) CC (Simon and Bailey)	2.56	89,456	33.80	26.51	61K	0.79	-28.73%
(3) MC ($\gamma = 0$)	2.49	85,370	34.28	27,86	n/a	0.77	-52.85%
(4) MC ($\gamma \in \{0.05, 0.1, 0.2\}$)	2.49	85,370	31.72	26.91	n/a	0.91	-23.77%
Comparison (2) vs. (4)	+	+	+	−	n/a	+	+

Table 6.11: Comparison of MC (with positive credibility) and CC (with balancing). "+": MC performs better than CC, "−": CC outperforms MC, "n/a": not applicable

larly, we follow the evolution of classification systems suggested by the course of our investigation; i.e. we look at

(1) CC without balancing

(2) CC including balancing (method of Simon and Bailey)

(3) MC without taking credibility into account ($\gamma = 0$)

(4) MC with positive credibility ($0 < \gamma (\leq 1)$).

Unfortunately, one cannot compute $crit_5$ for MC due to divisions by zero. $crit_6$ represents the *unweighted* version of the correlation coefficient. As far as $crit_7$ is concerned, one has to take $\hat{\pi}_\mathcal{K} = 3^{-1} \cdot 126.86$. Table 6.11 provides our results and contains a comparison of CC and MC.

Apparently, neither MC nor CC yield a positive variance reduction ($crit_6 < 0$ for both schemes). This effect is not uncommon, cf. the results in [Ajn86] for insurance of property and buildings.

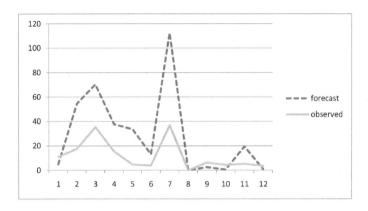

Figure 6.10: MC – actual and predicted claims expenditures

6.6 Discussion and Outlook

This section is devoted to discussing our empirical results and to an outlook where we identify some interesting problems and ideas for further research. First of all, as far as the data basis is concerned, table 6.11 retroactively justifies our construction of the collective since we are able to demonstrate common effects, namely improvements when including a balance method (predominantly better criteria from step (1) to step (2)) or the inclusion of credibility (improvements from (3) to (4)). This suggests the acceptability of the data basis.

More interestingly, we have empirically shown the superiority of MC compared to CC (improvements from (2) to (4) apart from only one criteria). This awareness is the core result of our investigation and confirms the theoretical properties of MC.

We also tested higher values of the credibility factor, e.g. $\gamma = 0.5$. However, such choices of γ led to significantly worse

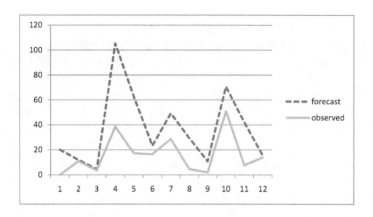

Figure 6.11: CC – actual and predicted claims expenditures

values of the criteria than calculated above. As already pointed out, we interprete the parameter γ as a measure of the fulfilment of the laws of large numbers. Apparently, the best criteria values are obtained for a credibility of 20%. This (low) figure suggests that the collective's atomic cells have merely a low degree of credibility.

Though we had to restrict ourselves to the case of only two charateristics, MC can be generalized to the case of more than two rating variables in a straight forward manner. If we are given at least three rating variables, the supersets which are necessary for computing credibility premiums can be chosen differently from our approach. Remember we chose – in the case of two variables – $x_{i.}$ and $x_{.j}$ as the "complement of credibility". If there are more than two attributes, one could sharpen this as follows: Instead of looking at $x_{i..}$, $x_{.j.}$, $x_{..k}$, we could – in the sense of an even more precise estimation – consider $x_{.jk}$, $x_{i.k}$, $x_{ij.}$.

Critics could be tempted to argue that MC must *eo ipso* perform better than our conception of CC since MC takes more information (namely atomic cell information) into account than CC does. Indeed, *atomic* cell information is meaningless for our CC system. However, their argument is unsustainable since we *do* consider cell information very well in the framework of CC, namely when balancing the claims expenditures by applying the method of Simon and Bailey. On the other hand, the consideration of cell values in CC schemes justifies to select a *positive* credibility factor in the MC approach. So we have a one-time consideration of cell claim information in either case.

Table 5.3.1 and also figure 6.10 show that MC normally performs very well – predicted premiums are fairly close to actually observed claims expenditures. There are, however, a few clusters showing considerable deviations between forecasted and actual premiums. Possibly, there are not enough risks to reveal the effects of the laws of large numbers. This suggests to test other classifications as well. For instance, one could vary important classification parameters like the number of tariff classes (reduction) or the minimum cluster size (increasement). While the variation of the number of tariff classes does not pose any technical problem, choosing cluster cardinalities is – in terms of a technical realization – more problematic. However, the algorithm proposed by [BG04] allows even such inputs beforehand.

So far, we have applied one common credibility factor to all atomic cells. In this setting, cell-specific characteristics (like exposure) do not play a role. However, actuarial literature has proposed a wide variety of credibility factors depending on concrete cell data some of which were presented here. Therefore, we recommend further research in the framework of applying several cell-specific credibility factors to MC.

Appendix A

Data

A.1   Random Number Generator

```java
import javax.swing.*;
public class Zufall
{
 static int klasse=0;
 static int zufall=0;
 static String s="1";
 static void berechnung(int klasse)
{
if (klasse == 1)
 zufall = (int)(Math.random()*1000*klasse);
if (klasse == 2)
 zufall = (int)(Math.random()*3999*klasse/2+1001);
if (klasse == 3)
 zufall = (int)(Math.random()*14999*klasse/3+5001);
}
public static void main(String[] args)
{
   System.out.println("Zum Beenden Schadenklasse
   0 angeben");
```

```
while(s!=null){
 String s = JOptionPane.showInputDialog("Schadenhoehen-
 klasse eingeben!");
klasse = Integer.parseInt(s);
if (klasse>3 || klasse<0)
   throw new IllegalArgumentException("Nicht zulaessig");
   if (klasse==0)
System.exit(0);
 else berechnung(klasse);
System.out.println(zufall);
  }
}
}
```

A.2 Claim Data

Tables A.1, A.2, A.3 and A.4 contain claim data as supported by ZMK (rank, age) and the generated claim sizes.

No.	rank	age	claim size (Euro)
1	HB	48	691
2	M	38	2834
3	M	45	817
4	M	46	305
5	HF	43	136
6	HF	39	1688
7	HF	46	4758
8	M	40	522
9	HF	37	252
10	SF	51	841
11	H	47	388
12	H	45	537
13	HB	29	2468
14	OG	21	531
15	HG	23	3658
16	HG	22	120
17	HG	23	787
18	OG	22	2356
19	OG	20	17475
20	OG	20	11121
21	OG	22	369
22	G	21	399
23	OG	21	555
24	G	19	165
25	G	19	212
26	OG	21	797
27	G	22	12758
28	OG	22	573
29	OG	21	4833
30	OG	21	3907
31	OG	22	728
32	OG	20	539
33	OF	27	4735
34	F	28	4486
35	OF	28	4304
36	OL	30	479
37	HG	24	730
38	HG	23	823
39	SG	25	379
40	SU	26	448
41	SU	27	5413
42	OL	31	4416
43	HG	23	590
44	HG	25	246
45	HG	23	460
46	H	31	621
47	HG	24	407
48	SU	22	725
49	U	25	13496
50	SG	26	3633

(continued on next page)

A.3 Composition and Claims Expenditure of the Collective

Tables A.6, A.8 and A.10 represent the exposures, the total claim sizes, the claims expenditures as for the atomic cells and the number of claims, respectively.

No.	rank	age	claim size (Euro)
51	OG	22	276
52	SU	23	18530
53	HG	24	772
54	OF	30	3410
55	F	29	2450
56	U	22	197
57	SU	26	155
58	HG	22	461
59	HG	26	894
60	SU	25	302
61	SU	29	401
62	HG	21	351
63	HF	35	801
64	HG	23	16128
65	HG	20	272
66	OF	29	2830
67	SU	27	1771

Table A.1: Reported accidents in January 2007

No.	rank	age	claim size (Euro)
1	M	35	643
2	SF	45	274
3	H	46	3094
4	HF	43	3644
5	OSB	51	1295
6	M	47	4811
7	OFA	47	1059
8	HF	40	4753
9	OF	30	2721
10	M	40	512
11	HF	36	415
12	OSF	53	388
13	M	33	2411
14	HF	38	426
15	HG	21	796
16	OG	22	758
17	HG	22	4685
18	OG	23	3599
19	G	20	2995
20	OG	21	940
21	G	20	960
22	G	19	693
23	OG	21	2797
24	OG	22	397
25	SU	26	2658
26	U	29	1399
27	OL	27	3323
28	OF	27	1556
29	OF	25	686
30	OG	25	208
31	SG	23	992
32	HG	22	4750
33	SU	26	868
34	F	26	706
35	HG	24	4225
36	HG	23	3289
37	U	27	1109
38	HG	22	2970
39	SU	26	569
40	OF	31	3846
41	HG	20	4751
42	SU	23	3952
43	HG	22	865
44	SU	26	15168
45	HG	23	363
46	HG	22	9067
47	SG	23	4696
48	SU	23	4622
49	SU	24	257
50	SG	24	5725
51	SG	26	842

Table A.2: Reported accidents in February 2007

No.	rank	age	claim size (Euro)
1	O	59	763
2	HF	37	396
3	HF	30	1925
4	HB	37	11090
5	H	50	641
6	HF	36	1533
7	SH	53	114
8	SF	47	3482
9	OSF	51	344
10	SF	48	284
11	HF	43	635
12	HF	43	611
13	M	48	553
14	SF	50	460
15	OF	31	461
16	HG	23	825
17	HG	22	2594
18	OG	19	566
19	OG	20	372
20	HG	22	14956
21	OG	23	1709
22	HG	20	4200
23	OG	19	270
24	OG	20	354
25	OG	21	551
26	OG	21	16375
27	SU	27	192
28	SU	23	1730
29	SU	27	388
30	HG	24	341
31	OSV	43	4500
32	OL	31	1294
33	SG	26	2240
34	OF	35	200
35	SG	24	4695
36	SU	27	427
37	HG	24	14982
38	OF	28	720
39	OL	28	629
40	SU	28	15155
41	SU	34	778
42	SG	23	766
43	SG	25	2257
44	HG	24	502
45	F	23	548
46	SG	23	538
47	HG	21	716
48	HG	23	722
49	OF	26	3807
50	HG	21	675
51	SG	33	253

Table A.3: Reported accidents in June 2007

No.	rank	age	claim size (Euro)
1	OTL	40	151
2	OTL	41	299
3	H	43	1414
4	H	36	380
5	HG	24	704
6	OG	19	3732
7	OG	22	943
8	OF	32	3265
9	OG	20	4585
10	HG	23	748
11	HG	20	784
12	OG	20	337
13	OG	21	3214
14	OG	20	390
15	OG	22	2668
16	OG	20	421
17	OB	30	331
18	SU	23	4128
19	B	22	633
20	HG	24	1614
21	HG	21	198
22	OF	29	161
23	H	34	496
24	OSG	28	726
25	SG	26	689
26	L	24	516
27	HG	22	538
28	OF	28	488
29	KL	29	319
30	OF	31	872
31	OF	25	992
32	SG	24	1997
33	HG	22	585
34	HG	22	287
35	SU	27	550
36	OG	21	4829
37	SU	22	644
38	HG	24	2743
39	SG	23	548
40	OF	23	976
41	HG	23	4202
42	OL	28	272
43	SU	24	2981

Table A.4: Reported accidents in July 2007

	O	OTL	M	SH	H	OL	L	OSF	SF	HF
61	1	0	0	0	0	0	0	0	0	0
60	1	0	0	0	0	0	0	0	0	0
59	2	2	0	0	0	0	0	0	0	0
58	1	4	0	0	0	0	0	0	0	0
57	1	4	0	1	0	0	0	0	0	0
56	1	4	0	1	0	0	0	0	0	0
55	2	4	0	1	0	0	0	0	0	0
54	2	5	0	1	5	0	0	1	1	0
53	1	5	0	1	5	0	0	7	11	0
52	1	5	0	0	5	0	0	6	10	0
51	1	6	0	1	7	0	0	9	12	1
50	1	7	0	0	8	0	0	8	12	2
49	1	7	1	0	7	0	0	7	11	4
48	1	7	2	0	7	1	0	7	13	6
47	0	8	2	0	8	1	0	6	13	5
46	0	7	2	0	7	1	0	4	11	6
45	0	7	2	0	7	1	0	2	11	6
44	0	6	1	0	6	1	0	1	10	7
43	0	6	2	0	5	1	0	0	8	13
42	0	5	2	0	5	2	0	0	5	12
41	0	5	3	0	4	2	0	0	3	15
40	0	4	6	0	3	3	0	0	1	18
39	0	3	4	0	2	4	0	0	0	18
38	0	3	5	0	2	4	1	0	0	19
37	0	2	4	0	2	4	2	0	0	22
36	0	2	4	0	3	3	3	0	0	22
35	0	2	4	0	4	2	3	0	0	21
34	0	2	2	0	6	1	3	0	0	22
33	0	2	2	0	8	2	2	0	0	23
32	0	1	2	0	10	3	2	0	0	24
31	0	1	2	0	13	7	2	0	0	22
30	0	1	2	0	10	8	2	0	0	17
29	0	0	2	0	5	11	3	0	0	9
28	0	0	1	0	1	15	6	0	0	3
27	0	0	1	0	0	12	9	0	0	1
26	0	0	0	0	0	5	15	0	0	0
25	0	0	0	0	0	1	18	0	0	1
24	0	0	0	0	0	0	13	0	0	1
23	0	0	0	0	0	0	6	0	0	1
22	0	0	0	0	0	0	1	0	0	0
21	0	0	0	0	0	0	0	0	0	0
20	0	0	0	0	0	0	0	0	0	0
19	0	0	0	0	0	0	0	0	0	0
sum	17	127	58	6	155	95	91	58	132	321

(continued on next page)

OF	F	SU	U	OSG	SG	HG	OG	G	sum
0	0	0	0	0	0	0	0	0	1
0	0	0	0	0	0	0	0	0	1
0	0	0	0	0	0	0	0	0	4
0	0	0	0	0	0	0	0	0	5
0	0	0	0	0	0	0	0	0	6
0	0	0	0	0	0	0	0	0	6
0	0	0	0	0	0	0	0	0	7
0	0	0	0	0	0	0	0	0	15
0	0	0	0	0	0	0	0	0	30
0	0	0	0	0	0	0	0	0	27
0	0	0	0	0	0	0	0	0	37
0	0	0	0	0	0	0	0	0	38
0	0	0	0	0	0	0	0	0	38
0	0	0	0	0	0	0	0	0	44
0	0	0	0	0	0	0	0	0	43
0	0	0	0	0	0	0	0	0	38
0	0	0	0	0	0	0	0	0	36
0	0	0	0	0	0	0	0	0	32
0	0	0	0	0	0	0	0	0	35
0	0	0	0	0	0	0	0	0	31
0	0	0	0	0	0	0	0	0	32
1	0	0	0	0	0	0	0	0	36
1	0	0	0	0	0	0	0	0	32
2	0	0	0	0	0	0	0	0	36
4	0	1	0	0	0	0	0	0	41
6	0	1	0	0	0	0	0	0	44
10	0	1	0	0	0	0	0	0	47
16	0	3	0	0	0	0	0	0	55
29	1	4	0	0	1	0	0	0	74
39	2	8	0	1	1	0	0	0	93
49	3	15	0	1	1	0	0	0	116
54	5	27	0	1	2	1	0	0	130
51	10	45	2	1	3	1	0	0	143
45	13	65	2	1	5	3	0	0	160
35	15	82	6	2	12	5	0	0	180
22	19	83	9	1	23	17	2	1	197
11	18	70	15	1	28	44	7	2	216
4	17	62	19	1	21	84	33	8	263
1	18	53	22	0	13	105	74	22	315
0	10	31	25	0	3	86	97	44	297
0	1	13	19	0	0	48	71	83	235
0	0	2	7	0	0	16	39	68	132
0	0	0	1	0	0	1	9	16	27
380	132	566	127	10	113	411	332	244	3,375

Table A.6: The composition of the collective $\mathcal{K}$

	O	OTL	M	SH	H	OL	L	OSF	SF	HF
61	0	0	0	0	0	0	0	0	0	0
60	0	0	0	0	0	0	0	0	0	0
59	763	0	0	0	0	0	0	0	0	0
58	0	0	0	0	0	0	0	0	0	0
57	0	0	0	0	0	0	0	0	0	0
56	0	0	0	0	0	0	0	0	0	0
55	0	0	0	0	0	0	0	0	0	0
54	0	0	0	0	0	0	0	0	0	0
53	0	0	0	114	0	0	0	388	0	0
52	0	0	0	0	0	0	0	0	0	0
51	0	0	0	0	0	0	0	1,639	841	0
50	0	0	0	0	641	0	0	0	460	0
49	0	0	0	0	0	0	0	0	0	0
48	0	0	553	0	0	0	0	0	284	691
47	0	1,059	4,811	0	388	0	0	0	3,482	0
46	0	0	305	0	3,094	0	0	0	0	4,758
45	0	0	817	0	537	0	0	0	274	0
44	0	0	0	0	0	0	0	0	0	0
43	0	0	4,500	0	0	0	0	0	0	5,026
42	0	0	0	0	0	0	0	0	0	0
41	0	0	0	0	0	0	0	0	0	0
40	0	0	1,034	0	0	0	0	0	0	4,753
39	0	0	0	0	0	0	0	0	0	1688
38	0	0	2,834	0	0	0	0	0	0	426
37	0	0	0	0	0	0	0	0	0	11,738
36	0	0	0	0	0	0	0	0	0	1,948
35	0	0	643	0	0	0	0	0	0	801
34	0	0	0	0	0	0	0	0	0	0
33	0	0	2,411	0	0	0	0	0	0	0
32	0	0	0	0	0	0	0	0	0	0
31	0	0	0	0	621	5,710	0	0	0	0
30	0	0	0	0	0	479	0	0	0	1,925
29	0	0	0	0	0	0	0	0	0	2,468
28	0	0	0	0	0	629	0	0	0	0
27	0	0	0	0	0	3,323	0	0	0	0
26	0	0	0	0	0	0	0	0	0	0
25	0	0	0	0	0	0	0	0	0	0
24	0	0	0	0	0	0	0	0	0	0
23	0	0	0	0	0	0	0	0	0	0
22	0	0	0	0	0	0	0	0	0	0
21	0	0	0	0	0	0	0	0	0	0
20	0	0	0	0	0	0	0	0	0	0
19	0	0	0	0	0	0	0	0	0	0
sum	763	1,059	17,908	114	5,281	10,141	0	2,027	5,341	36,222

(continued on next page)

OF	F	SU	U	OSG	SG	HG	OG	G	sum
0	0	0	0	0	0	0	0	0	0
0	0	0	0	0	0	0	0	0	0
0	0	0	0	0	0	0	0	0	763
0	0	0	0	0	0	0	0	0	0
0	0	0	0	0	0	0	0	0	0
0	0	0	0	0	0	0	0	0	0
0	0	0	0	0	0	0	0	0	0
0	0	0	0	0	0	0	0	0	0
0	0	0	0	0	0	0	0	0	502
0	0	0	0	0	0	0	0	0	0
0	0	0	0	0	0	0	0	0	2,480
0	0	0	0	0	0	0	0	0	1,101
0	0	0	0	0	0	0	0	0	0
0	0	0	0	0	0	0	0	0	1,528
0	0	0	0	0	0	0	0	0	9,740
0	0	0	0	0	0	0	0	0	8,157
0	0	0	0	0	0	0	0	0	1,628
0	0	0	0	0	0	0	0	0	0
0	0	0	0	0	0	0	0	0	9,526
0	0	0	0	0	0	0	0	0	0
0	0	0	0	0	0	0	0	0	0
0	0	0	0	0	0	0	0	0	5,787
0	0	0	0	0	0	0	0	0	1,688
0	0	0	0	0	0	0	0	0	3,260
0	0	0	0	0	0	0	0	0	11,738
0	0	0	0	0	0	0	0	0	1,948
200	0	0	0	0	0	0	0	0	1,644
0	0	778	0	0	0	0	0	0	778
0	0	0	0	0	253	0	0	0	2,664
0	0	0	0	0	0	0	0	0	0
4,307	0	0	0	0	0	0	0	0	10,638
6,131	0	0	0	0	0	0	0	0	8,535
2,830	2,450	401	1,399	0	0	0	0	0	9,548
5,024	4,486	15,155	0	0	0	0	0	0	25,294
6,291	0	8,191	1,109	0	0	0	0	0	18,914
3,807	706	19,866	0	0	6715	894	0	0	31,988
686	0	302	13,496	0	2,636	246	208	0	17,574
0	0	257	0	0	10,420	21,959	0	0	32,636
0	548	28,834	0	0	6,992	27,645	5,308	0	69,327
0	0	725	197	0	0	40,468	5,457	12,758	59,605
0	0	0	0	0	0	2,538	30,489	1,196	34,223
0	0	0	0	0	0	9,223	29,861	3,955	43,039
0	0	0	0	0	0	0	836	1,070	1,906
29,276	8,190	74,509	16,201	0	27,016	102,973	72,159	18,979	428,159

Table A.8: Total claim sizes

	O	OTL	M	SH	H	OL	L	OSF	SF	HF
61	0.0	–	–	–	–	–	–	–	–	–
60	0.0	–	–	–	–	–	–	–	–	–
59	381,5	0.0	–	–	–	–	–	–	–	–
58	0.0	0.0	–	–	–	–	–	–	–	–
57	0.0	0.0	–	0.0	–	–	–	–	–	–
56	0.0	0.0	–	0.0	–	–	–	–	–	–
55	0.0	0.0	–	0.0	–	–	–	–	–	–
54	0.0	0.0	–	0.0	0.0	–	–	0.0	0,0	–
53	0.0	0.0	–	114.0	0.0	–	–	55.4	0.0	–
52	0.0	0.0	–	–	0.0	–	–	0.0	0.0	–
51	0.0	0.0	–	0.0	0.0	–	–	182.1	70.1	0.0
50	0.0	0.0	–	–	80.1	–	–	0.0	38.3	0.0
49	0.0	0.0	0.0	–	0.0	–	–	0.0	0.0	0.0
48	0.0	0.0	276.5	–	0.0	0.0	–	0.0	21.9	115.2
47	–	132.4	2405.5	–	48.5	0.0	–	0.0	267.9	0.0
46	–	0.0	152.5	–	442.0	0.0	–	0.0	0.0	793.0
45	–	0.0	408.5	–	76.7	0.0	–	0.0	24.9	0.0
44	–	0.0	0.0	–	0.0	0.0	–	0.0	0.0	0.0
43	–	0.0	2250.0	–	0.0	0.0	–	–	0.0	386.6
42	–	0.0	0.0	–	0.0	0.0	–	–	0.0	0.0
41	–	0.0	0.0	–	0.0	0.0	–	–	0.0	0.0
40	–	0.0	172.3	–	0.0	0.0	–	–	0.0	264.1
39	–	0.0	0.0	–	0.0	0.0	–	–	–	93.8
38	–	0.0	566.8	–	0.0	0.0	0.0	–	–	22.4
37	–	0.0	0.0	–	0.0	0.0	0.0	–	–	533.6
36	–	0.0	0.0	–	0.0	0.0	0.0	–	–	88.6
35	–	0.0	160.8	–	0.0	0.0	0.0	–	–	38.1
34	–	0.0	0.0	–	0.0	0.0	0.0	–	–	0.0
33	–	0.0	1205.5	–	0.0	0.0	0.0	–	–	0.0
32	–	0.0	0.0	–	0.0	0.0	0.0	–	–	0.0
31	–	0.0	0.0	–	47.8	815.7	0.0	–	–	0.0
30	–	0.0	0.0	–	0.0	59.9	0.0	–	–	113.2
29	–	–	0.0	–	0.0	0.0	0.0	–	–	274.2
28	–	–	0.0	–	0.0	41.9	0.0	–	–	0.0
27	–	–	0.0	–	–	276.9	0.0	–	–	0.0
26	–	–	–	–	–	0.0	0.0	–	–	
25	–	–	–	–	–	0.0	0.0	–	–	0.0
24	–	–	–	–	–	–	0.0	–	–	0.0
23	–	–	–	–	–	–	0.0	–	–	0.0
22	–	–	–	–	–	–	0.0	–	–	–
21	–	–	–	–	–	–	–	–	–	–
20	–	–	–	–	–	–	–	–	–	–
19	–	–	–	–	–	–	–	–	–	–
marginal	44.9	8.3	308.8	19.0	34.1	106.8	0.0	35.0	40.5	112.8

(continued on next page)

OF	F	SU	U	OSG	SG	HG	OG	G	marginal
–	–	–	–	–	–	–	–	–	0.0
–	–	–	–	–	–	–	–	–	0.0
–	–	–	–	–	–	–	–	–	190.8
–	–	–	–	–	–	–	–	–	0.0
–	–	–	–	–	–	–	–	–	0.0
–	–	–	–	–	–	–	–	–	0.0
–	–	–	–	–	–	–	–	–	0.0
–	–	–	–	–	–	–	–	–	0.0
–	–	–	–	–	–	–	–	–	16.7
–	–	–	–	–	–	–	–	–	0.0
–	–	–	–	–	–	–	–	–	67.0
–	–	–	–	–	–	–	–	–	28.9
–	–	–	–	–	–	–	–	–	0.0
–	–	–	–	–	–	–	–	–	34.7
–	–	–	–	–	–	–	–	–	226.5
–	–	–	–	–	–	–	–	–	214.7
–	–	–	–	–	–	–	–	–	45.2
–	–	–	–	–	–	–	–	–	0.0
–	–	–	–	–	–	–	–	–	272.2
–	–	–	–	–	–	–	–	–	0.0
–	–	–	–	–	–	–	–	–	0.0
0.0	–	–	–	–	–	–	–	–	160.8
0.0	–	–	–	–	–	–	–	–	52.8
0.0	–	–	–	–	–	–	–	–	90.6
0.0	–	–	–	–	–	–	–	–	286.3
0.0	–	0.0	–	–	–	–	–	–	44.3
20.0	–	0.0	–	–	–	–	–	–	35.0
0.0	–	259.3	–	–	–	–	–	–	14.2
0.0	0.0	0.0	–	–	253.0	–	–	–	36.0
0.0	0.0	0.0	–	0.0	0.0	–	–	–	0.0
87.9	0.0	0.0	–	0.0	0.0	–	–	–	91.7
113.5	0.0	0.0	–	0.0	0.0	0.0	–	–	65.7
55.5	245.0	8.9	699.5	0.0	0.0	0.0	–	–	66.8
111.6	345.1	233.2	0.0	0.0	0.0	0.0	–	–	158.1
179.7	0.0	99.9	184.8	0.0	0.0	0.0	–	–	105.1
173.1	37.2	239.4	0.0	0.0	292.0	52.6	0.0	0.0	162.4
62.4	0.0	4.3	899.7	0.0	94.1	5.6	29.7	0.0	81.4
0.0	0.0	4.2	0.0	0.0	496.2	261.4	0.0	0.0	124.1
0.0	30.4	544.0	0.0	–	537.9	263.3	71.7	0.0	220.1
–	0.0	23.4	7.9	–	0.0	470.6	56.3	290.0	200.7
–	0.0	0.0	0.0	–	–	52.9	429.4	14.4	146,0
–	–	0.0	0.0	–	–	576.4	765.7	58.2	326.1
–	–	–	0.0	–	–	0.0	92.9	66.9	70.6
77.0	62.1	131.6	127.6	0.0	239.1	250.5	217.4	77.8	126.9

Table A.10: Claims expenditures

181

Bibliography

[Ajn86] B. Ajne: Comparison of some methods to fit a multiplicative tariff structure to observed risk data, *ASTIN Bulletin* 16 (1986), 63-68.

[AL88] P. Albrecht, S. Lippe: Prämie, mathematische und wirtschaftliche Fragen, in: *Handwörterbuch der Versicherung* (Eds. D. Farny, E. Helten, P. Koch, R. Schmidt), Verlag Versicherungswirtschaft, 1988.

[Alb81] P. Albrecht: Kredibilität, Erfahrungstarifierung und sekundäre Prämiendifferenzierung, in: *Geld, Banken und Versicherungen* (Eds. H. Göppl, R. Henn), Athenäum, 1981.

[Alb82] P. Albrecht: Gesetze der großen Zahlen und Ausgleich im Kollektiv – Bemerkungen zu Grundlagen der Versicherungsproduktion, *Zeitschrift für die gesamte Versicherungswissenschaft* 71 (1982), 501-538.

[Alb84a] P. Albrecht: Ausgleich im Kollektiv und Prämienprinzipien, *Zeitschrift für die gesamte Versicherungswissenschaft* 73 (1984), 167-180.

[Alb84b] P. Albrecht: Welche Faktoren begünstigen den Ausgleich im Kollektiv?, *Zeitschrift für die gesamte Versicherungswissenschaft* 73 (1984), 181-201.

[Alb87] P. Albrecht: Ausgleich im Kollektiv und Verlust-wahrscheinlichkeit, *Zeitschrift für die gesamte Versicherungswissenschaft* 76 (1987), 95-117.

[And73] M. R. Anderberg: *Cluster Analysis for Applications*, Academic Press, 1973.

[AS88] P. Albrecht, E. Schwake: Risiko, Versicherungstechnisches, in: *Handwörterbuch der Versicherung* (Eds. D. Farny, E. Helten, P. Koch, R. Schmidt), Verlag Versicherungswirtschaft, 1988.

[Bac96] J. Bacher: *Clusteranalyse*, Oldenbourg, 2. ed. 1996.

[Bai63] R. A. Bailey: Insurance Rates with Minimum Bias, *Proceedings of the Casualty Actuarial Society L* (1963), 4-11.

[Bau92] H. Bauer: *Maß- und Integrationstheorie*, Walter der Gruyter, 2. ed. 1992.

[Bau02] H. Bauer: *Wahrscheinlichkeitstheorie*, Walter de Gruyter, 5. ed. 2002.

[BCHJKPR05] P. Booth, R. Chadburn, S. Haberman, D. James, Z. Khorasanee, R. Plumb, B. Rickayzen: *Modern Actuarial Theory and Practice*, Chapman & Hall/CRC, 2005.

[BDMGLM91] J. Beirlant, V. Derveaux, A. M. De Meyer, M. J. Goovaerts, E. Labie, B. Maenhoudt: Statistical risk evaluation applied to (Belgian) car insurance, *Insurance: Mathematics and Economics* 10 (1991), 289-302.

[Ber81] S. Bergs: *Optimalität bei Clusteranalysen*, Dissertation, Westfälische Wilhelms-Universität Münster, 1981.

[BG04] A. Brieden, P. Gritzmann: A quadratic optimization model for the consolidation of farmland by means of lend-lease agreements, in: *Operations research Proceedings 2003: Selected Papers of the International Conference on Operations Research (OR 2003)* (Eds. D. Ahr, R. Fahrion, M. Oswald, G. Reinelt), Springer, 2004.

[BG07] A. Brieden, P. Gritzmann: Von Ackerbau und polytopalen Halbnormen: Diskrete Optimierung für die Landwirtschaft, in: *Kombinatorische Optimierung erleben* (Eds. S. Hußmann, B. Lutz-Westphal), vieweg, 2007.

[BHW75] P. L. Butzer, W. Hahn, U. Westphal: On the rate of approximation in the central limit theorem, *Journal of Approximation Theory* 13 (1975), 327-340.

[BN75] M. Beuthe, P. van Namen: La sélection des assurés et la détermination des primes d'assurances par l'analyse discriminante, *Mitteilungen der Vereinigung schweizerischer Versicherungsmathematiker* 1975, 137-156.

[Boc74] H. H. Bock: *Automatische Klassifikation*, Vandenhoeck & Rupprecht, 1974.

[Boc94] H. H. Bock: Classification and Clustering: Problems for the Future, in: *New Approaches in Classification and Data Analysis* (Eds. E. Diday, Y. Lechevallier, M. Schader, P. Bertrand, B. Burtschy), Springer, 1994.

[Boe71] C. Boehm: Das Faktoren- und das Summanden-Modell, *Blätter der Deutschen Gesellschaft für Versicherungsmathematik* 10 (1971), 3-33.

[Boo89] A. Boos: Anwendungen der Credibility-Theorie in der Kraftfahrzeughaftpflichtversicherung, in: *Beiträge zur Credibility-Theorie* (Ed. E. Helten), Verlag Versicherungswirtschaft, 1989.

[Boo91] A. Boos: *Effizienz von Bonus-Malus-Systemen*, Gabler Verlag, 1991.

[BS60] R. A Bailey, L. J. Simon: Two studies in automobile insurance ratemaking, *ASTIN Bulletin* 1 (1960), 192-217.

[BS70] H. Bühlmann, E. Straub: Glaubwürdigkeit für Schadensätze, *Mitteilungen der Vereinigung schweizerischer Versicherungsmathematiker* (1970), 111-133.

[Bue67] H. Bühlmann: Experience Rating and Credibility, *ASTIN Bulletin* 4 (1967), 199-207.

[Bue70] H. Bühlmann: *Mathematical Methods in Risk Theory*, Springer, 1970.

[BW92] M. J. Brockman, T. S. Wright: Statistical Motor Rating: Making Effective Use of Your Data, *Journal of the Institute of Actuaries* 119 (1992), 457-526.

[Cam86] M. Campbell: An Integrated System for Estimating the Risk Premium of Individual Car Models in Motor Insurance, *ASTIN Bulletin* 16 (1986), 165-183.

[CF79] L. Chang, W. B. Fairly: Pricing Automobile Insurance under Multivariate Classification of Risks: Additive versus Multiplicative, *The Journal of Risk and Insurance* 46 (1979), 75-93.

[DG85] O. Deprez, H. U. Gerber: On convex principles of premium calculation, *Insurance: Mathematics and Economics* 4 (1985), 179-189.

[Dic78] H. Dickmann: Einsatz der Clusteranalyse bei Klassifikationsproblemen in der Versicherungswirtschaft, *Blätter der Deutschen Gesellschaft für Versicherungsmathematik* 13 (1978), 378-401.

[DO95] R. A. Derrig, K. M. Ostaszewski: Fuzzy Techniques of Pattern Recognition in Risk and Claim Classification, *The Journal of Risk and Insurance* 62 (1995), 447-482.

[DPP94] C. D. Daykin, T. Pentikäinen, M. Pesonen: *Practical Risk Theory for Actuaries*, Chapman & Hall/CRC, 1994.

[Ede92] D. B. Edelman: An application of cluster analysis in credit control, *IMA Journal of Mathematics Applied in Business & Industry* 4 (1992), 81-87.

[EG70] E. J. Elton, M. J. Gruber: Homogeneous Groups and the Testing of Economic Hypotheses, *Journal of Financial and Quantitative Analysis* 4 (1970), 581-602.

[EG71] E. J. Elton, M. J. Gruber: Improved Forecasting through the Design of Homogeneous Groups, *The Journal of Business* 44 (1971), 432-450.

[Ete81] N. Etemadi: An elemantary proof of the strong law of large numbers, *Probability Theory and Related Fields* 55 (1981), 119-122.

[Eve93] B. S. Everitt: *Cluster Analysis*, Edward Arnold, 3. ed. 1993.

[Fel04] S. Feldblum: Risk Classification, Pricing Aspects, in: *Encyclopedia of Actuarial Science* (Eds. J.L. Teugels, B. Sundt), 2004.

[FIM01] A. Foglia, S. Iannotti, P. Marullo Reedtz: The Definition of the Grading Scales in Banks' Internal Rating Systems, *Economic Notes* 30 (2001), 421-456.

[Fin04] R. Finger: Risk Classification, Practical Aspects, in: *Encyclopedia of Actuarial Science* (Eds. J.L. Teugels, B. Sundt), 2004.

[Fis05] G. Fischer: *Lineare Algebra*, vieweg, 15. ed. 2005.

[Fis76] M. Fisz: *Wahrscheinlichkeitsrechnung und mathematische Statistik*, Deutscher Verlag der Wissenschaften, 1976.

[For06] O. Forster: *Analysis 2*, vieweg, 7. ed. 2006.

[FP80] G. M. Frankfurter, H. E. Phillips: Portfolio selection: an analytic approach for selecting securities from a large universe, *Journal of Financial and Quantitative Analysis* 15 (1980), 357-377.

[FTW81] : W. B. Fairley, T. J. Tomberlin, H. I. Weisberg: Pricing Automobile Insurance under a Cross-Classification of Risks: Evidence from New Jersey, *The Journal of Risk and Insurance* 48 (1981), 505-514.

[GDV08a] http://www.versicherung-und-verkehr.de/index.php/
1;cmid;6;crid;45, accessed 13.7.2008

[GDV08b] http://www.gdv-dl.de/typklassenverzeichnis.html, accessed 2.9.2008.

[GDV08c] Gesamtverband der Deutschen Versicherungswirtschaft e.V.: *Statistisches Taschenbuch der Versicherungswirtschaft 2008.*

[GDV08d] Gesamtverband der Deutschen Versicherungswirtschaft e.V.: *GDV-Positionen* 63 (2008).

[GDV09] http://www.gdv.de/Themen/Querschnittsthemen/- RechtsundVerbraucherfragen/Beruecksichti-gung_des_Geschlechts_bei_der_Kalkula-tion_von_Versicherungsvertraegen/inhalts-seite22105.html, accessed 18.1.2009.

[Ger79] H. U. Gerber: *An Introduction to Mathematical Risk Theory*, S. S. Huebner Foundation, 1979.

[GS77] P. Gänssler, W. Stute: *Wahrscheinlichkeitstheorie*, Springer, 1977.

[GVH84] M. Goovaerts, F. de Vylder, J. Haezendonck: *Insurance Premiums*, North-Holland, 1984.

[Hei87] W.-R. Heilmann: *Grundbegriffe der Risikotheorie*, Verlag Versicherungswirtschaft, 1987.

[Hei88] W.-R. Heilmann: Schadenversicherungsmathematik, in: *Handwörterbuch der Versicherung* (Eds. D. Farny, E. Helten, P. Koch, R. Schmidt), Verlag Versicherungswirtschaft, 1988.

[Hel74] E. Helten: Statistische Probleme der Tarifierung in der Kraftfahrthaftpflichtversicherung, *Zeitschrift für die gesamte Versicherungswissenschaft* 63 (1974), 153-177.

[Hel78] E. Helten: Klassifizierungsprobleme bei der Neuordnung der Regionalstruktur des Kraftfahrzeug-Haftpflichtversicherungtarifs, *Blätter der Deutschen Gesellschaft für Versicherungsmathematik* 13 (1978), 375-385.

[HH97] D. J. Hand, W. E. Henley: Statistical Classification Methods in Consumer Credit Scoring: a Review, *Journal of the Royal Statistical Society* 160 (1997), 523-541.

[HK01] M. Heep-Altiner, M. Klemmstein: *Versicherungsmathematische Anwendungen in der Praxis – mit Schwerpunkt Kraftfahrt und Allgemeine Haftpflicht*, Verlag Versicherungswirtschaft, 2001.

[HKT90] C. Hsiao, C. Kim, G. Taylor: A Statistical Perspective on Insurance Rate Making, *Journal of Econometrics* 44 (1990), 5-24.

[HN03] S. E. Harrington, G. R. Niehaus: *Risk Management and Insurance*, McGraw-Hill, 2. ed. 2003.

[Hob03] R. Hoberg: *Clusteranalyse, Klassifikation und Datentiefe*, Dissertation, Universität zu Köln, 2003.

[Hof99] P. Hofmeister: Customer Segmentation with Fuzzy Clustering, in: *Soft Computing in Financial Engineering (Studies in Fuziness and Soft Computing* 28 (1999)) (Eds. R. A. Ribeiro, H.-J. Zimmermann, R. R. Yager, J. Kacprzyk).

[INZ05] J. Iwanik, J. Nowicka-Zagrajek: Premiums in the Individual and Collective Risk Models, in: *Statistical Tools for Finance and Insurance* (Eds. P. Cizek, W. Härdle, R. Weron), Springer, 2005.

[Jac83] K. Jacobs: *Einführung in die Kombinatorik*, Walter de Gruyter & Co., 1983.

[Jaj98] K. Jajuga: Classification and Data Analysis in Finance, in: *Data Science, Classification, and Related Methods* (Eds. C. Hayashi, N. Ohsumi, K. Yajima, Y. Tanaka, H. H. Bock, Y. Baba), Springer, 1998.

[Jee89] B. Jee: A Comparative Analysis of Alternative Pure Premium Models in the Automobile Risk Classification System, *Journal of Risk and Insurance* 56 (1989), 434-459.

[Jen71] R. E. Jensen: A Cluster Analysis Study of Financial Performance of Selected Business Firms, *The Accounting Review* 46 (1971), 36-56.

[Jun68] J. Jung: On automobile insurance ratemaking, *ASTIN Bulletin* 5 (1968), 41-48.

[KGDD01] R. Kaas, M. Goovaerts, J. Dhaene, M. Denuit: *Modern Actuarial Risk Theory*, Kluwer Academic Publishers, 2001.

[KL75] Y. Kahane, H. Levy: Regulation in the Insurance Industry: Determination of Premiums in Automobile Insurance, *Journal of Risk and Insurance* 42 (1975), 117-132.

[KPW04] S. A. Klugman, H. H. Panjer, G. E. Willmot: *Loss Models: From Data to Decisions*, Wiley, 2. ed. 2004.

[Kre99] E. Kremer: *Applied Risk Theory*, Shaker, 1999.

[Kro71] C. O. Kroncke: The Process of Classifiying Drivers: A Suggestion for Insurance Ratemaking, *The Journal of Risk and Insurance* 38 (1971), 543-551.

[Kru97] O. Kruse: *Modell zur Analyse und Prognose des Schadenbedarfs in der Kraftfahrzeug-Haftpflichtversicherung*, Verlag Versicherungswirtschaft, 1997.

[KW01] J. P. Krahnen, M. Weber: Generally Accepted Rating Principles: A Primer, *Journal of Banking and Finance* 25 (2001), 3-23.

[Lem77] J. Lemaire: Selection procedures of regression analysis applied to automobile insurance, *Mitteilungen der Vereinigung schweizerischer Versicherungsmathematiker* (1977), 143-160.

[Lem79] J. Lemaire: Selection procedures of regression analysis applied to automobile insurance, *Mitteilungen der Vereinigung schweizerischer Versicherungsmathematiker* (1979), 65-72.

[Lem85] J. Lemaire: *Automobile Insurance: Actuarial Models*, Kluwer Academic Publishers, 1985.

[LJL80] K. Loimaranta, J. Jacobsson, H. Lonka: On the Use of Mixture Models in Clustering Multivariate Frequency Data, *Transactions of the 21st International Congress of Actuaries* (1980), 147-161.

[Lun92] M. Lundy: Cluster Analysis in Credit Scoring, in: *Credit Scoring and Credit Control* (Eds. L. C. Thomas, J. N. Crook and D. B. Edelman), Clarendon, 1992.

[Mac02] T. Mack: *Schadenversicherungsmathematik*, Verlag Versicherungswirtschaft, 2. ed. 2002.

[Meh62] J. Mehring: Die Schadenstruktur in der Kraftfahrt-Haftpflichtversicherung von Personenwagen, *Blätter der Deutschen Gesellschaft für Versicherungsmathematik* 6 (1962), 23-41.

[Meh64] J. Mehring: Ein mathematisches Hilfsmittel für Statistik- und Tariffragen in der Kraftfahrthaftpflichtversicherung, *Blätter der Deutschen Gesellschaft für Versicherungsmathematik* 7 (1964), 111-125.

[Nor79] R. Norberg: The credibility approach to experience rating, *Scandinavian Actuarial Journal* (1979), 181-221.

[NRR95] B. Niggemeyer, M. Radtke, A. Reich: Applications of Risk Theory and Multivariate Analysis in Insurance Practice, *Applied Stochastic Models and Data Analysis* 11 (1995), 231-244.

[Rad08] M. Radtke: *Grundlagen der Kalkulation von Versicherungsprodukten in der Schaden- und Unfallversicherung*, Verlag Versicherungswirtschaft, 2008.

[Rau98] N. Rautmann: *Risikogerechte Prämienkalkulation im Versicherungsunternehmen am Beispiel der industriellen Feuerversicherung*, Dissertation, Universität Hamburg, 1998.

[Rej03] G. E. Rejda: *Principles of Risk Management and Insurance*, Addison Wesley, 8. ed. 2003.

[RHSS07] B. Rudolph, B. Hofmann, A. Schaber, K. Schäfer: *Kreditrisikotransfer – Moderne Instrumente und Methoden*, Springer, 2007.

[Sam86] D. Samson: Designing an automobile insurance classification system, *European Journal of Operational Research* 27 (1986), 235-241.

[San80] D. T. Sant: Estimating Expected Losses in Auto Insurance, *The Journal of Risk and Insurance* 47 (1980), 133-151.

[SC89] K. J. Stroinski, I. D. Currie: Selection of variables for automobile insurance rating, *Insurance: Mathematics and Economics* 8 (1989), 35-46.

[Sch85] K.-A. Schäffer: Klassifizierung regionaler Schadenbedarfsunterschiede für PKW in der Kraftfahrzeug-Haftpflichtversicherung, *Zeitschrift für die gesamte Versicherungswissenschaft* 74 (1985), 1-19.

[Sch06] K. D. Schmidt: *Versicherungsmathematik*, Springer, 2. ed. 2006.

[Sie71] H. Sievers: Die Entwicklung der Struktur in der Kraftfahrt-Haftpflicht-Versicherung, *Blätter der Deutschen Gesellschaft für Versicherungsmathematik* 10 (1971), 165-173.

[Sie88] H. Sievers: Kraftfahrzeug-Haftpflichtversicherung, in: *Handwörterbuch der Versicherung* (Eds. D. Farny, E. Helten, P. Koch, R. Schmidt), Verlag Versicherungswirtschaft, 1988.

[SL77] D. Steinhausen, K. Langer: *Clusteranalyse – Einführung in Methoden und Verfahren der automatischen Klassifikation*, Walter de Gruyter & Co., 1977.

[Spä77] H. Späth: *Cluster-Analyse-Algorithmen*, Oldenbourg, 1977.

[Spä83] H. Späth: *Cluster-Formation und -Analyse – Theorie, FORTRAN-Programme, Beispiele*, Oldenbourg, 1983.

[SS77] D. Steinhausen, J. Steinhausen: Cluster-Analyse als Instrument der Zielgruppendefinition in der Marktforschung, in: *Fallstudien Cluster-Analyse* (Ed. H. Späth), Oldenbourg, 1977.

[ST87] D. Samson, H. Thomas: Linear Models as Aids in Insurance Decision Making: The Estimation of Automoble Insurance Claims, *Journal of Business Research* 15 (1987), 247-256.

[Ste83] H. P. Sterk: Statistik als Instrument der Risikopolitik, *Zeitschrift für die gesamte Versicherungswissenschaft* 72 (1983), 231-254.

[Sti80] K. Sticker: *Analyse der Tarifstruktur für die Haftpflichtversicherung von Personenkraftwagen*, Verlag Versicherungswirtschaft, 1980.

[Sti82] K. Sticker: Zur Kalkulation der Kraftfahrt-Haftpflicht-Tarife: Erstellung und Aufbereitung der Gesamtstatistik, *Zeitschrift für die gesamte Versicherungswissenschaft* 71 (1982), 27-45.

[Str88] E. Straub: *Non-Life Insurance Mathematics*, Springer, 1988.

[SWB00] K. A. Smith, R. J. Wills, M. Brooks: An analysis of customer retention and insurance claim patterns using data mining: a case study, *Journal of the Operational Research Society* 51 (2000), 532-541.

[Tro77] A. Tröbliger: Analyse und Prognose des Schadenbedarfs für die Kraftfahrthaftpflichtversicherung für Pkw, *Blätter der Deutschen Gesellschaft für Versicherungsmathematik* 13 (1977), 1-26.

[Try80] P. Tryfos: On Classification in Automobile Insurance, *The Journal of Risk and Insurance* 47 (1980), 331-337.

[vEGN83] J. v. Eeghen, E. K. Greup, J. A. Nijssen: *Survey of Actuarial Studies: Rate Making*, Nationale-Nederlanden N.V., 1983.

[vENR82] J. v. Eeghen, J. A. Nijssen, F. A. M. Ruygt: Interdependence of Risk Factors: Application of Some Models, *New Motor Rating Structure in the Netherlands*, ASTIN-groep, 105-119.

[Vog75] F. Vogel: *Probleme und Verfahren der numerischen Klassifikation – unter besonderer Berücksichtigung von Alternativmerkmalen*, Vandenhoeck & Ruprecht in Göttingen, 1975.

[Völ08] M. Völklein: Kampf ums Kfz, *Süddeutsche Zeitung*, 22./23.11.2008.

[vSc89] A. v. Schaaffhausen: Grundlagen der Credibility-Theorie, in: *Beiträge zur Credibility-Theorie* (Ed. E. Helten), Verlag Versicherungswirtschaft, 1989.

[Wal98] J. T. Walter: *Zur Anwendung von Verallgemeinerten Linearen Modellen zu Zwecken der Tarifierung in der Kraftfahrzeug-Haftpflichtversicherung*, Verlag Versicherungswirtschaft, 1998.

[Web96] R. Weber: Customer Segmentation for Banks and Insurance Groiups with Fuzzy Clustering Techniques, in: *Fuzzy Logic* (Ed. J. F. Baldwin), Wiley, 1996.

[Wei87] H. Weiß: *Automatische Klassifikation von Unfällen als Verfahren der Unfallforschung*, Dissertation, Bergische Universität Gesamthochschule Wuppertal, 1987.

[WH97] G. J. Williams, Z. Huang: Mining the Knowledge Mine: The Hot Spots Methodology for Mining Large Real World Databases, *Lecture Notes in Artifical Intelligence* 1342 (1997), 340-348.

[Whi18] A. W. Whitney: The theory of experience rating, *Proceedings of the Casualty Actuarial Society* 4 (1918), 274-292.

[WHP03] B. Wolf, M. Hill, M. Pfaue: *Strukturierte Finanzierungen*, Schäffer-Poeschel, 2003.

[Wit86] G. W. de Wit: Risk theory, a tool for management?, in: *Insurance and Risk Theory* (Eds. M. Goovaerts, F. de Vylder, J. Haezendonck), 1986.

[WSY98] C. A. Williams, M. L. Smith, P. C. Young: *Risk Management and Insurance*, McGraw-Hill, 8. ed. 1998.

[WT82] H. Weisberg, T. Tomberlin: A Statistical Perspective on Actuarial Methods for Estimating Pure Premiums From Cross-Classified Data, *The Journal of Risk and Insurance* 49 (1982), 539-563.

[WTC84] H. Weisberg, T. Tomberlin, S. Chatterjee: Predicting Insurance Losses Under Cross-Classification: A Comparison of Alternative Approaches, *Journal of Business and Economic Statistics* 2 (1984), 170-178.

[YSWB01] A. C. Yeo, K. A. Smith, R. J. Wills, M. Brooks: Clustering Technique for Risk Classification and Prediction of Claim Costs in the Automobile Insurance Industry, *International Journal of Intelligent Systems in Accounting, Finance and Management* 10 (2001), 39-50.

[YSWB03] A. C. Yeo, K. A. Smith, R. J. Wills, M. Brooks: A comparison of soft computing and traditional approaches for risk classification and claim cost prediction in the automobile insurance industry, in: *Soft Computing in Measurement and Information Acquisition, Studies in Fuzziness and Soft Computing* (Eds. L. Reznik and V. Kreinovich), vol. 127, Springer-Verlag, Chapter 18, 249-261, 2003.

[Zim80] R. Zimmermann: Die Verfahrensweise der Kalkulationsstatistik in der Kraftfahrt-Haftpflichtversicherung,

Veröffentlichungen des Bundesaufsichtsamtes für das Versicherungs- und Bausparwesen 29 (1980), 198-207.

Schriften zum Controlling, Finanz- und Risikomanagement

Herausgegeben von Prof. Dr. Andreas Brieden, Prof. Dr. Thomas Hartung,
Prof. Dr. Bernhard Hirsch und Prof. Dr. Andreas Schüler

Band 1 Patrick Siklóssy: Vergleich der Durchführungswege der betrieblichen Altersversorgung aus Eigentümer- und Arbeitnehmersicht. 2009.

Band 2 Simon Krotter: Performance-Messung, Erwartungsänderungen und Analystenschätzungen. Theoretische Konzeption und empirische Umsetzung. 2009.

Band 3 Hans-Jürgen Straßer: DCF-Bewertung von Versicherungsunternehmen. 2009.

Band 4 Bernhard Christian Kübler: Risk Classification by Means of Clustering. 2010.

www.peterlang.de